FOR SUCH A
TIME AS THIS

FOR SUCH A TIME AS THIS

Dr. Fuchsia T. Pickett

Destiny Image Publishers
P.O. Box 310
Shippensburg, PA 17257-0310

"Speaking to the Purposes
of God for this Generation"

ISBN 1-56043-078-8

For Worldwide Distribution
Printed in the U.S.A.

Cover art: Suzanne Adams Hubbard

Acknowledgments

I am deeply grateful to Revs. Morris and Lydia Taylor of Love International, Santa Anna, California for their financial gift to provide a computer to help in the publishing of my books.

My sincere appreciation to Cheryl Tipon, Nancy Quinn, Patricia L. Riggs, and Carol Noe, who have helped me gather my teaching and preaching of the revelation of the Book of Esther over a period of years into a readable form. It is with their help that I could write this prophetic message to the Church.

Dedication

To my son, Darrell, who relinquished so much of his life with his mother in order for her to train leaders and to minister to the body of Christ in both the local church and the Church at large.

Contents

Foreword xi

Introduction xiii

Chapter   **Page**
1   **The Allegory**
         The Church in Type 1

2   **Historical Events**
         The Church in Time 15

3   **The Characters**
         The Church in Temptation 29

4   **The Preparation of Esther**
         The Church in Trials 41

5   **The Reign of Queen Esther**
         The Church in Trouble 55

6   **The Courage of Esther**
         The Church in Threatenings 67

7   **Esther Exposes Haman**
         The Church in Worship 79

8   **Kingdom Rule Established**
         The Church Triumphant 91

Foreword

For years the lines have been drawn between Bible interpreters who embrace the use of types, shadows, images and allegories as legitimate forms of Bible exegesis and those who insist on a strictly historical interpretation. To those who allegorize, this book is a treasure chest of truth. While Dr. Pickett confines her allegories to the Book of Esther, she touches a broad area of Christian living.

I have known Dr. Pickett for over thirty years. Few Bible teachers can handle types and shadows as forcefully as she. She is well studied in the entire Bible and is greatly experienced both as a teacher and a preacher. This book, *For Such a Time as This*, is among her best allegorical studies. I have seen its message hold participants at conventions spellbound for several days.

For those who fear this approach to Bible interpretation, the book can shed some needed light. Dr. Pickett does not build doctrine on Old Testament types—she uses them to illustrate clearly defined doctrine and truth of the New Testament. To her, the Old Testament abounds with illustrations that illuminate spiritual principles, much as a preacher's stories make the sermon come alive.

Whether or not you can see yourself as an Esther or an Ahasuerus, this book will make the Book of Esther take on a new meaning for you.

Judson Cornwall, Th.D.
Phoenix, Arizona

Introduction

I have realized that "the Church," who is neither an organization, location nor institution, but that "called out" living organism that has come from the very mind and heart of God Himself, is no afterthought in God's purposes. Though the revelation of the Church in the Old Testament is concealed in its types and with picturesque figurative language, it is fully revealed in the New Testament as the culmination of God's eternal plan.

I have become very grateful for the revelation by the Holy Spirit of the prophetic picture found in the Book of Esther. The narrative shares the glorious triumph of the Church, her relationship with the Holy Spirit, her victory over the flesh and her relationship with the King of Kings as she learns how to prepare a worship feast for Him.

The Book of Esther is perhaps one of the greatest prophetic books in the Bible regarding the Church. It gives us tremendous insight into where the Church is today in relation to the purposes of God. Since it is not a book that is taught very often, all many people know about it is the lovely historical story that it is, emphasizing the theme that Esther was brought to the kingdom "for such a time as this."

I suggest that the Book of Esther be reread along with the reading of this book. May it help us in finding the purposes of God for our lives and in fulfilling our destiny for our generation.

Dr. Fuchsia Pickett
April, 1992

1

The Allegory

The Church in Type

The Book of Esther is one of the greatest prophetic books of the Bible. That statement may surprise those who have read Esther only as a historical account of dramatic events that threatened the lives of God's chosen people. It is true that the story of Esther is an accurate chronicle that teaches the providence of God in caring for His people. But its message is not limited to an understanding of these historical events. God is trying to communicate much more than natural happenings in the Book of Esther. Throughout the Scriptures God uses natural circumstances to teach eternal truths, revealing an infinite God to finite humans. His yearning to reveal Himself to mankind is so strong that

1

He goes to great lengths, using life itself to teach us principles regarding His love.

When the infinite God desired to communicate with finite men, He had to find ways for us to understand what He was saying. Because of sin, men's minds could not comprehend a God who was holy and absolute. So God reached into our world and used human language to reveal His will for mankind. He spoke to men through parables, metaphors, similes, hyperboles, types and allegories. Using these linguistic tools, God unfolded beautiful truths about Himself and His purposes for mankind in His Word.

The story of Esther, as an example, reveals to us through allegory and type deep truths concerning our relationship with God and His plan for the Church. Esther is a type of the Church within the Church. She represents the bride of Christ who is being prepared to come into the Presence of the King of Kings. As we watch the process of preparation to which she must submit, we can see the Church allegorically in this hour. We can learn the ways of God in His dealings with His Church to purify her and bring her into His Presence. The ultimate destruction of Esther's enemies and the subsequent rule of righteousness and peace give us hope for today. In the midst of our personal testings we can believe that what God ordained for His Church He is able to accomplish. He will have a Church "without spot or wrinkle," one purified through testings who will worship the Father "in spirit and in truth." A true understanding of the Book of Esther prophetically reveals to us that glorious Church for which Jesus Christ died.

A careful foundation must be laid for the understanding of type and allegory so that we do not violate the true meaning of the Scriptures. A *type* is a person, thing or event that represents another, especially another that is to come in the future. Typology, the study of types, can bring to light many precious truths in the Word of God that are otherwise hidden to us. We can discover these truths as silver is discovered: by descending into a dark mine shaft and digging for them. An *allegory* is a story in which people, things and happenings have a symbolic significance, not merely a literal one, that is often morally instructive.

When Jesus taught about the shepherd who searched for his lost sheep, He was not telling the story of a specific event that happened in Galilee. He was using that natural illustration of a shepherd's care for his sheep to show the Father's love and care for each of His children. David portrayed the Lord as a Shepherd in the poetic psalm that has spoken comfort to us throughout the centuries. How beautifully these word pictures help to reveal the nature of God to us! In the Old Testament, when animal sacrifices were initiated to atone for men's sins, God was foreshadowing prophetically the sacrifice of His Son at Calvary, the one death that would accomplish the reality of atonement. Those sacrifices were a type of the reality of Jesus' sacrifice to come.

THREE MAJOR TYPES

There are three main types, or "skeletons," that walk through the Book and unlock its truth from Genesis to Revelation. Following these pictures through the Bible provides a beautiful understanding of God's plan for His Church. The first of these types is the picture of the Tabernacle or Temple. David's Tabernacle and Solomon's Temple reveal to us beautiful aspects of the worship that God desires. The Lord is intent on creating a temple of worship to bring into His Presence. Paul admonishes believers, "Know ye not that ye are the temple of God?" (I Cor. 3:16) As New Testament Christians, each of us has become a habitation for the Spirit of God, a temple of worship where the King is to be enthroned.

A second type that unlocks the Book is the picture of the human body or anatomy. The Bible depicts Christians as the body of Christ in the earth. Paul exhorts the Corinthians that they are "members in particular" of the body of Christ, and that God has set everyone in the body as it has pleased Him (I Cor. 12:18,27).

The analogy of the bride and bridegroom is a third type that unlocks eternal truths throughout Scripture.

Rebekah, Ruth and Esther give us beautiful insight into our relationship to Jesus Christ. God is preparing a bride for His Son to bring to the wedding feast of the Lamb.

So God communicates eternal truths through "picture language." We learn to look beyond the natural elements of truth in Scripture to receive the deeper allegorical truths they teach. The Temple, the body of Christ and the bride of Christ are pictures that can be used like road maps to lead us ultimately to revelation of our heavenly Father, unfolding truth concerning Himself and His purposes for mankind. We can read the Bible for its literal history of recorded events or from a philosophical standpoint. Not opening our minds, however, to parables, parabolic expressions, similes, metaphors, types and allegories will cause us to miss much of the understanding of what God is saying in His Word.

To properly understand type and allegory, we must realize that it is important not to attempt to make every word in a story fit a divine truth. There will usually be one or two spiritual truths to uncover from the otherwise natural event. We must be careful not to try to find types in every intricate detail of an allegory that was written to reveal a few major truths. No earthly story completely symbolizes an eternal truth. For example, Abraham represents God the Father in Scripture. Yet we see that Abraham sometimes did not act like God. Because of his humanity, he could not be a perfect type of the heavenly Father. Joseph is perhaps the most complete type of Christ in the Bible. There are over three hundred comparisons between his life and the life of Christ. But he was not a perfect man. These men did live out certain truths, however, in their natural lives that help us receive a spiritual message from a spiritual country and King.

We also must make sure that the truth revealed in the type can go through the cross. That is to say, the truth it teaches must relate without question to God's eternal plan for the salvation of mankind that was fulfilled through the shedding of Jesus' blood on Calvary. Each truth that is concealed in a type in the Old Testament is revealed in the New Testament reality of Jesus' sacrifice for the sin of mankind. Only as types and allegories help us to apply truth to our lives, and as they agree with all other Scripture, are they valid revelation. The ultimate purpose for all revelation must be to transform us into the image of Christ.

In the beautiful allegory of Esther we discover some rich eternal truths. We have acknowledged the historical veracity of the events found in the Book of Esther. The Jewish people still celebrate some of those events today. However, as an allegory, the Book of Esther more clearly illustrates the principles of the life of Christ that must govern the life of the believer than any other single book in the Old Testament. Nowhere else is there demonstrated more plainly the spiritual new birth experience. The Book of Esther clearly explains the conditions that must be met before we may enter the Presence of the King. It gives us a beautiful understanding of bringing the Church into true worship. Esther also teaches us truths concerning true discipleship, that which involves giving all so that we might follow Him.

An unusual trait of the Book of Esther is that the Name of God is not found in it. Still, we witness the providence of God throughout the book of Esther, and we see how He takes care of His people in adversity. We also learn through Esther how God humbles the proud and exalts the lowly, and that He saves those who pray to Him and trust in Him. As we look carefully behind the historical facts of the places and characters found in the Book of Esther, we will discover these beautiful truths God was revealing to mankind. In His attempt to reveal His love to man, God used the real lives of people as tools of communication to help us comprehend an infinite God. Though events were significant in themselves, we will find meaningful allegorical truths as well that we can apply to our walk with God.

TWO MAJOR STREAMS OF REVELATION

There are two allegorical streams of revelation in the Book of Esther, and each is complete in itself.

These two facets of truth complement each other. The revelation of the *tripartite nature of man* in its redemptive process flows side by side with the *prophetic revelation of the Church*. These two allegorical streams finally merge into one great river in the reality of "Christ in you, the hope of glory." By studying each stream carefully, we will be enriched in our understanding of God's ways as He deals with mankind. His ultimate purpose is to have a glorious Church without spot or wrinkle, filled with Christians who have been purified to worship Him in spirit and in truth.

THE NATURE OF MAN REDEEMED

The first stream of revelation in Esther teaches the redemption of the tripartite nature of man. It reveals the source of personal conflict for the born-again Christian. Through our understanding of that conflict, we can learn to overcome the power of sin that threatens to destroy us. God created man as a spirit with a soul and body. When Adam sinned, his spirit, which had been alive to God, died to that relationship. He began to be ruled by his soul, which consists of the intellect, will and emotions. Living in independence from God brought death to mankind—a death God had never intended that man experience. When we accept the provision of the blood of Christ for sin and are born again, our spirits are recreated. We become alive to God and enter into relationship with Him.

That relationship is not complete, however, until our souls are perfectly surrendered to God. The way we think and feel, the decisions we make by our wills, must come under the control of the Holy Spirit for us to enjoy the righteousness, peace and joy of His Kingdom. That kind of surrender does not happen overnight, but requires a continual process of yielding to the work of the Holy Spirit. Conflict is inevitable when we find our wills, thoughts or affections running contrary to God's.

Understanding the tripartite nature of man and the conflict caused by the sin problem, we follow this allegorical stream through Esther to see how God deals with an individual to bring him to the crisis of the born-again experience. In the first part of our story, the king represents the *soul* of man. That part of man that lives on the throne is responsible ultimately for all our decisions. Our wills rule our decisions and govern our intellect and emotions. God has given every man a free will by which we may choose to love God or to reject Him. God's desire is to receive love from a willing heart that chooses to give allegiance to God alone. The king we see as the story opens is ruling his own kingdom independently, having no relationship with God.

The queen, Vashti, represents the *independent, rebellious spirit* of man that refuses to obey or to cooperate with the king. She must be put away so that Esther, the *submissive, born-again spirit,* can come to the palace. Esther has a family relationship with Mordecai and obeys him in all things. Mordecai typifies the *Holy Spirit,* whose rulership always brings peace and prosperity to the kingdom. Haman represents the *flesh,* or the natural nature of man. Haman has great influence with the king, or soul, and always rivals the Holy Spirit for honor, demanding preeminence. Haman will not tolerate Mordecai, whom he hates. Because of his hatred, he determines to rid the earth of Mordecai and all Jews. He viciously attacks the life of Esther, threatening not only her life, but that of her people, who represent the *Church.* The intensity of the conflict between Haman and Esther allows no hope for coexistence.

This human conflict accurately describes the reality of the struggle of every born-again believer. Our natural life wars against the life of the Spirit of God within us. The New Testament states that reality clearly when Paul writes to the Galatians, "For the flesh lusteth against the Spirit, and the Spirit against the flesh: and these are contrary the one to the other..." (Gal. 5:17) To the Romans Paul explains, "For they that are after the flesh do mind the things of the flesh; but they that are after the Spirit, the things of the Spirit. For to be carnally minded is death; but to be spiritually minded is life and peace" (Rom. 8:5-6). We can rejoice in the deliverance of Esther from Haman, expecting to enjoy the same victory in our personal lives as we yield to the work of the Holy Spirit.

THE CHURCH PROPHETICALLY REVEALED

The second major stream of revelation concerns the prophetic revelation of the Church in Esther. It teaches us of God's desire for His Church to come into His Presence in true worship and reveals the process involved to bring her there. Following this allegorical stream, we see God preparing His bride and redeeming His Church to fulfill His purposes. We watch His providential care for His people and see how He gives victory over the enemies that threaten the Church.

The king in this case represents Jesus, our Bridegroom. Of course, the king we see in the opening of the story does not fit this allegorical stream. Jesus is the ruler of the Kingdom in which Mordecai has been given proper authority and all his enemies destroyed. When the Holy Spirit has taken His rightful place in the Church, we will know peace from our enemies and the reign of righteousness, peace and joy in the Kingdom of God.

Esther, the obedient queen and bride, represents the Church within the Church. She is the bride who has chosen to live in a love relationship with the King without regard to the suffering required to qualify her for that relationship. It was Esther's obedience to Mordecai and her willingness to lay down her life for her people that resulted in the saving of all their lives in the end. The secret of Esther's obedient heart is reflected in her statements: *"If it please the king..."* and *"If I perish, I perish."* The Church must express this same twofold cry in order to be saved from her enemies. We must desire to please the King of Kings in all we do. And we must be willing to lay down our lives, that righteousness may prevail over wickedness. This is the testimony of the Church in the Book of the Revelation: "And they overcame him by the blood of the Lamb, and by the word of their testimony; and they loved not their lives unto the death" (Rev. 12:11).

The preparations of Esther to come into the presence of the king reveal the processes of God for bringing the Church into His Presence. They parallel as well the dealings of God for the individual believer who is being made ready to come before the Presence of the King. There is no contradiction between the dealings of God with individual believers and those preparations for His Church, the body of Christ in the earth. The Church is made up of believers who have allowed the dealings and preparations of God to become a life-changing reality.

Following these two streams of revelation from this rich allegory, we can approach the setting of the book with greater expectation, not merely looking at natural places and events. We can expect to see the way God works to redeem man, as well as His purpose to establish His Church in the earth. As we allow the Holy Spirit to quicken our minds to the allegorical significance of the places, characters and events, we will discover truths of the love of God and His determination to reveal that love to mankind.

2

Historical Events

The Church in Time

God limits Himself to time and place to fulfill His eternal plan for His Church. Yet these limitations do not hinder God in carrying out His purposes. He uses them to His advantage to prepare hearts to enter His great Kingdom of love. His patience is inexhaustible as He ordains providential circumstances to create crises that will bring men to a place of choice. The workmanship of God in His people is of far greater value than we can ever realize until we see from the perspective of eternity.

THE TIME

In *God's Dream* I wrote of the hurt-love of God that made Him willing to sacrifice His only Son to satisfy

the desire of His heart for a family. My description of
how God has used time to fulfill His desire is worth
reviewing here to give us an eternal perspective of
God's plan for His Church. I wrote:

> The most wonderful love story ever told is the
> story of God's love. All mankind is part of God's
> dream for a family, "according as He hath
> chosen us in Him before the foundation of the
> world...having predestinated us unto the adop-
> tion of children by Jesus Christ to Himself, ac-
> cording to the good pleasure of His will..."
> (Eph. 1:4-5).

> Having purposed to fulfill His dream for a fami-
> ly in spite of the cost, God began to unfold His
> eternal plan by cutting an eon in half and calling
> it time. He began His work of creation and set
> mankind in the Garden of Eden. There He fel-
> lowshipped with the first ones He created to be-
> come the family that would satisfy His heart of
> love and fulfill His dream. But Adam and his
> wife failed the love test through their dis-
> obedience. The Voice came walking, seeking
> him. "Adam, where are you?" Still the Father's
> dream, known only to the Godhead, was not
> revealed to man. God couldn't tell Adam of the
> covenant of the Godhead because of his dis-
> obedience.

> Centuries later, Moses received the law of God,
> but that law could not tell us what God's dream

was. That which was in God's heart—His dream—was not revealed. The historians, psalmists and poets of the Bible did not perceive it. Even the prophets were not aware of God's dream. Four hundred dark years after the prophets were silent, what God had planned was not yet revealed.

So God cut out His love in the form of a Person and sent Him to earth as the express image of God. Everything Jesus did, each word He spoke, was to show us the Father's heart. Jesus healed the sick and set the captives free to reveal to us the Father's love....

Even Jesus could not tell His disciples what was in the Father's heart. They had centered their thoughts on a present earthly kingdom....

Jesus completed the plan for the redemption of mankind through His sacrifice on Calvary. The Holy Spirit was then entrusted to do His precious work in the earth to draw men to God.... The throb of God's heart was still to have a family in His image, with His family spirit—the Spirit of the Lamb—to live and rule with Him. However, no one had yet been able to declare that dream fully to us. On the day of Pentecost, when the Holy Spirit came, Peter put his telescope to the entire Church Age, but he didn't see the whole dream of God. He saw bits of its beginning and ending as he prophesied (Acts chapter two), but he didn't say a word about what was in the Father's heart.

Then one day, a man with a slaughtering spirit, seemingly farther from the heart of God than anyone could be, had a supernatural encounter with the living God, and was apprehended for a special purpose. Saul of Tarsus was converted and became Paul, the apostle. He was a "full gospel preacher" for a while, until God told him to go to the desert of Arabia. Without conferring with flesh and blood, he obeyed the Spirit's command. During the three years Paul spent in that desert, the Father unfolded to him the mystery that had been hidden since before the foundation of the world.

Paul explained to the church at Ephesus that God's eternal plan was "...to make plain to everyone the administration of this mystery, which for ages past was kept hidden in God...His intent was that now, through the church, the manifold wisdom of God should be made known to the rulers and authorities in the heavenly realms, according to His eternal purpose which He accomplished in Christ Jesus our Lord" (Eph. 3:9-11, NIV). God was going to realize His dream for a family through the Church, the body of Christ on the earth.[1]

Though God dwells in eternity, He works in time to fulfill His divine purposes. God is the Husbandman who "waiteth for the precious fruit of the earth..." (James 5:7) For nearly two thousand years He has been patiently laboring in the earth to build His Church. Throughout the centuries He has been restoring truths that the Church lost following its magnificent early days as recorded in the Book of Acts. We are going to see His handiwork in the fulness of time, culminating in a glorious Church and in the presentation of a beautiful bride for His Son.

The psalmist cried out, "My times are in Thy hand: deliver me from the hand of mine enemies..." (Ps. 31:15) As we see the Church in type in Esther, we witness the spiritual conflict that is set against her. She has to face formidable enemies by putting her trust in God alone to save her. Can we appreciate the pathos and passion of Mordecai's plea to Esther? "...and who knoweth whether thou art come to the kingdom for such a time as this?" (Esther 4:14) Esther's eternal destiny was revealed in one moment of crisis that would decide both her fate and that of her people.

A study of Church history reveals many other terrible conflicts the Church has endured as her enemies have sought to destroy her. Yet today the Church is being strengthened and is getting ready for a move of God such as we have never seen. We can expect to see today the same kind of victory over wickedness as that

Esther experienced for her people. God is preparing His Esther again to reign triumphantly, completely submitted to the authority of the Holy Spirit. He will have a glorious Church formed in time to reign with Him in eternity.

THE PLACE

The place God chose as the setting for the major events of the story of Esther was the royal city of Shushan. The name *Shushan* means "lily city." In Scripture the lily represents a bride. For example, in the Song of Solomon, the Shulamite girl told the daughters of Jerusalem that her beloved had gone to the garden to gather lilies. She continued, "I am my beloved's, and my beloved is mine: he feedeth among the lilies." The bridegroom was preparing for a wedding in the garden of lilies. God said Israel would "blossom like a lily," when referring to her as a faithful bride to Him (Hos. 14:4-5, NAS). In the Hebrew language, the words for the lily and the almond bloom are the same. The only flower that God used in the Tabernacle was the almond bloom that He instructed to be engraved in the Holy of Holies. The artisans fashioned the candelabra to look like lilies, foreshadowing the bride He desires to bring into His Presence.

Jesus told His disciples to consider the lilies of the field, how they grow. He said, "They toil not, neither do they spin: and yet...even Solomon in all his glory was not arrayed like one of these. Wherefore, if God so

clothe the grass of the field, which today is and tomorrow is cast into the oven, shall He not much more
clothe you, O ye of little faith?" (Matt. 6:28-30) God
esteemed the lily more than the grandeur of Solomon's
Temple. We can read about the tons of gold used in the
building of Solomon's Temple, the yards of purple vel-
vet and the thousands of precious jewels. Yet these
riches did not impress God as much as did the beauty
of His handiwork in the lily of the field.

Considering the lilies will teach us truths about the
bride of Christ and about how God builds His
Kingdom. The works of God which we may consider
to be commonplace and of little value God esteems
more than all the greatest monuments man can build.
God's lilies are His people in whom He has wrought a
dependence and trust of rare beauty. We begin to understand that simple trusting relationship we are to
have with God Who alone can clothe us with the
beauty of the lily. So it is significant that Esther's
home, the setting for this allegory, is the "lily city." We
can expect to witness the work of God here creating
the beauty He desires in His people.

As the historical narrative opens, the writer intro-
duces us to a powerful king sitting upon his throne and
ruling over his vast empire. King Ahasuerus ruled
from India to Ethiopia over one hundred twenty-seven
provinces. The simple definition of the boundaries of
this empire gives us a perspective of the power and influence of King Ahasuerus as a world ruler. After he

had ruled for three years, the king made a feast for all his princes and servants. His purpose was to display the power and wealth of his kingdom.

For six months the feast continued. After that lengthy celebration, the king invited all the people who lived in Susa, the capital, to a feast that lasted seven days. The palace must have fascinated the people, with its exquisite hangings of white and purple linen, marble columns, and couches of gold and silver. The guests walked on pavements of red, blue, white and black marble, mother-of-pearl and precious stones. Everything they saw testified to the great wealth and power of this king. They enjoyed the beautiful monumental pillars in the Garden of Marble as they viewed the extravagant hangings that were an art form of that day.

As the guests were marveling at the splendor of the palace, they were given vessels of gold. These golden vessels were each of a unique style, handmade for a single purpose: to be filled with the king's wine. According to custom, the quantity of wine one consumed in the king's presence showed how much he honored the king and enjoyed his presence. Yet this king allowed his guests to drink as much or as little as they desired. He did not obligate them to drink to show him their gratitude for being in his presence.

Thinking allegorically about the unique gold vessels filled with wine, we can see how they speak of our life in Christ. Gold in Scripture represents the character of God in His deity and worth. The Ark of the Covenant, where God's Presence dwelt in Old Testament times, was overlaid in pure gold, and the Mercy Seat was made of pure gold. When we come to the throne of God in prayer to ask for mercy, we find the character of God there. In the purity of His love and kindness He is there to receive us. Wine is a picture of the Holy Spirit, the living breath of God. These unique gold vessels filled with wine are like the children of God in the earth, the Church. As God's children, we are all vessels designed to display the character of God and to be filled with His life. He will never force us to drink of His life, but wants us to choose to be partakers of the life of the Holy Spirit.

Jesus teaches us to abide as branches in the Vine so we will produce the fruit of the Vine. He is the Vine and we are the branches. As we allow His Word to abide in us and keep His commandments, we will bear much fruit. The character and nature of the vine produce the life flow of the branches. Jesus is the character of God living in us and producing fruit that will remain. The Church can be filled with the Presence of God if we will continually allow the character of God to be worked in us. The forming of that character will require us to humble ourselves as Jesus did to fulfill the will of the Father.

When kings of the Old Testament era wanted to humiliate a person, they offered him wine from an earthen vessel instead of a golden one. Everyone in the court knew that person had displeased the king. He was publicly humiliated by having to drink the king's wine from an earthen vessel. When Jesus came to earth, He willingly humbled Himself to leave eternity and pour Himself into an earthen vessel. He laid aside His deity and became a man, submitting Himself to the limitations of time and place. Through that humbling to become an earthen vessel filled with the character and life of God, He made possible our redemption through His death on the cross.

Paul declared to the Church that "we have this treasure in earthen vessels, that the excellency of the power may be of God" (II Cor. 4:7). The character of God as seen in the humility of Christ will be reflected in the Church. God wants to replace the humiliation of these earthen vessels with His character shining forth as gold in the lives of His children. That can only happen through a dramatic transformation of our human natures. In the exciting narrative of Esther, we see in type that supernatural transformation.

Reading the Book of Esther is like watching a fast-moving movie filled with intrigue, insubordination, romance and conflict. As events unfold, we can enjoy watching good win over evil and seeing righteousness triumph over wickedness in this historical account of God's intervention to save His people.

As the king's celebration continued, he encountered some unexpected difficulties. While King Ahasuerus was displaying the greatness and wealth of his kingdom, he decided to bring in his queen to show her off as well. To his consternation, Vashti the queen refused to come at the king's command. Because of this rebellious breach of protocol, the king sought counsel from those around him in deciding what should be done with a queen who expressed such insubordination to the king. The counsel he received was to banish his queen and to seek a new one. The king consented to that counsel, which resulted in his eventually choosing Esther, cousin of Mordecai the Jew, to become the new queen (Esther 2). As we watch Esther's obedience and submissive spirit during the process of being chosen queen and during her reign, we see the character of the bride of Christ.

The historical events recorded in the Book of Esther wonderfully reveal the providence of God as we watch the care with which He guards His people. God gives His children every opportunity of divine aid to triumph over the destructive forces that would swallow us. He is a mighty Deliverer who fights for His own, enabling us to do exploits against our enemies. The riches of divine truth that we discover in this simple narrative are a wonderful inspiration to every soul who feels the decree of death upon him. He can appeal to his King. By his simply making that appeal, his deliverance is sure.

As dramatic as the historical events are, they unfold even more significantly as we begin to explore the allegorical truths they represent. We can gain precious understanding of our individual Christian walk as well as of the prophetic revelation of the Church through our study. As an allegory, Esther is a story in which people, things and happenings have a depth of meaning. To explore that meaning, we can imagine ourselves descending into a silver mine to extract the precious ore of truth from beneath the surface of the earth. As we descend, we first discover the characters in the allegory. They reveal the nature of this kingdom to us as we explore the meanings of their names.

End Notes

1. Dr. Fuchsia Pickett, *God's Dream*, (Shippensburg, PA: Destiny Image, 1991), pp. 8-12. *God's Dream* is available at Christian bookstores or by writing to Dr. Fuchsia Pickett Ministries, 394 Glory Road, Blountville, TN 37617 ($7.00 per copy).

3

The Characters

The Church in Temptation

What's in a name? Our study of the name *Shushan* revealed its significance as the place where God was doing His handiwork. The "lily city" was the home of the bride and eventually came under the benevolent reign of peace and righteousness of the Holy Spirit. The names of people in the allegory can similarly unlock crucial truths concerning the character of this kingdom. Historically, children were given names that held meaning, not simply having a pleasant sound or honoring a favorite relative. Names often revealed the character of a person, especially in the Scriptures.

When God wrestled with Jacob, He asked him to declare his name. In saying his name, Jacob came to

the realization of his character, for his name means
supplanter, trickster, deceiver. In that terrible and
wonderful meeting with God, Jacob's name was
changed to match the change in his character that was
wrought through his dramatic encounter with the Lord.
The Name *Jesus* means *savior*. When the angel of the
Lord appeared to Joseph in a dream, He declared that
Joseph's espoused wife, Mary, would bring forth a Son
who was to be called Jesus, "for He shall save His
people from their sins." Understanding names in
Scripture is very important to our unlocking truth that
we would otherwise miss.

As the story of Esther opens we meet King
Ahasuerus, whose name means *mighty one*. He is a
stubborn, self-centered, dominating, egotistical
monarch who represents the unregenerate soul of a
man. The soul is the home of man's intellect, emotions
and will. The will of the king determines his decisions
for life. Similarly, out of the throne room of our souls
proceed the decrees for our lives. We are ultimately
responsible before God for every decision we make as
we exercise our free wills. Though others may seek to
influence us in our decisions, we choose whether we
will yield to their influences. God sets the choice of
life and death before us, and desires that we choose
life. If we do not, we must accept the consequences of
our decisions.

King Ahasuerus surrounded himself with seven
chamberlains who served in his presence, and other

wise men who knew the times. The king looked to these men for help in making decisions. Their names have meanings that are very revealing as to the character of the counsel this king received. Those to whom we give credence, allowing them to influence our decisions through their counsel, help to form our character. Whether our counsel comes from our own inner desires and thoughts or from people around us, it may sound similar to the voices of the men who surrounded this unregenerate king.

In the Church these same counselors are often heard, for unless the Holy Spirit has His proper place in the Church, we will be subject to the opinions, accusations and ideas of carnal minds. There are two sources of wisdom found in Scripture. One is wisdom from above, from the mind of God, that is "pure …peaceable, gentle, and easy to be entreated, full of mercy and good fruits, without partiality, and without hypocrisy" (James 3:17). The other source of wisdom is the one who "sealed up the sum of wisdom" before he was cast out of heaven to become the archenemy of God. Lucifer is the source of wisdom that is "earthly, sensual, devilish" (James 3:15). His wisdom produces envy, strife, confusion and every evil work (v. 16).

Of course, King Ahasuerus was receiving counsel from unregenerate men because he himself was unregenerate. The first chamberlain mentioned in this king's court was Mehuman, whose name means *faith-ful*, or, *I have been faithful*. This character may appear as a positive influence at first, until he places demands upon us because of his record of faithfulness. He may expect us to follow his suggestions because he has earned the right to be heard. If his voice is heard through friends and family, our loyalty to them could hinder our decisions for God. If his voice comes from within our own hearts, we should check to see if we are being loyal to ourselves rather than to God. Where we place our loyalties in times of decision will influence our futures in a powerful way.

Biztha, the next chamberlain mentioned, is closely related to the first. His name means *I have served you well, you owe me a lot*. If we show loyalty to ourselves or to others who demand such allegiance, we will not give proper allegiance to God. Harbona, whose name means *my own decisions*, was a powerful chamberlain. His name has a driving force to it, and suggests en-tanglement. Humanism, the atheistic religion of many, declares every person to be self-determining. That is, each is responsible for his destiny based solely on his decisions. This philosophy makes man autonomous, without regard to a divine source of power greater than himself. Such a deception works powerfully on the in-dependent mind of the king, causing him to deny the reality of God.

Bigtha inspires even more loyalty. His name means *in the winepress through many afflictions*. Suffering has a way of bonding people together. This can be positive when it strengthens us to do the will of God. However, if we feel obligated to respond to this character in ourselves or in others before considering the will of God, we are not wise. Abagtha, whose name means *father of the winepress*, is closely related to Bigtha. He takes credit for having made us what we are because of his investment in our lives; therefore, he must be considered in all our decisions.

Zethar is a most tempting chamberlain to follow. His name means *I'll bring you out on top*. He promises to make sure we are winners if we follow his suggestions and yield to his influence. There is in every person a desire to rule, to be in control of his life. Following the advice of this chamberlain to "come out on top" would directly oppose our Lord's teaching that to be great we must become the servants of all (Matt. 20:27).

Carcas, the last chamberlain mentioned, is a strong influence whose name means *bound one*. He insists that we are bound to him and cannot change, for we have been this way all our lives. Though we can all relate to a painful resistance within us to accepting change, we must not allow that reluctance to keep us from obeying God. We dare not bind ourselves to people, places or positions in a way that would keep us from following the call of God on our lives.

How often have we seen the Church lose the life of God because she resisted change and chose to honor tradition instead of receiving the new revelation God was restoring? We have become bound to doing things the way we always have and cannot accept the fresh life God breathes. So God's Spirit moves on to accomplish His purpose. I can think of nothing more tragic than to be in a church where God used to be. Many local churches have refused the fuller revelation of praise and worship that God is bringing to His body. They have listened to the counsel of Carcas, and are bound to the ways they have always had "church." We must be willing to change our ways, submitting them to the Holy Spirit, if we expect to grow in the life of God.

Coming under the influence of even one of these miserable chamberlains could defeat any desire one has for God. Taken together, they present a formidable foe as they assault our soul from without and within, form our loyalties and ultimately affect our decisions. Yet as powerful as these seven chamberlains were, they were not the only influential people to be found in the king's presence.

There were seven wise men in this historical king's court who held a higher position than the chamberlains did. Their power to influence the king was greater than that of the first counselors, and, allegorically, they hold greater power to influence our lives. The first wise man was named Carshena, meaning *Change thou the Lamb*. Scripture teaches clearly that sin can only be eliminated by the shed blood of a lamb. That fact culminated in the shedding of Christ's blood as the Lamb of God on Calvary. Yet in spite of that, throughout history segments of the Church have tried to deny the need for the blood of Jesus as the only atonement for sin. Others have desired a gospel of prosperity without suffering. Great religious movements that seem to be Christian, at least in name, have dared to eliminate the blood from their teachings as they come under the influence of "Change thou the Lamb." Theirs is an empty dogma that overlooks Scriptures such as Hebrews 9:22, "Without shedding of blood is no remission." Without the efficacious, vicarious, substitutionary, mediatorial work of the precious Lamb, man is without hope. The influence of this "wise" man keeps the king from the true knowledge and power of the gospel.

Next to Carshena sits Shethar, whose name means *I'll search out your answers*. With no knowledge of the true gospel, Shethar determines to find alternate answers for the king's questions regarding life. Philosophies such as atheism, humanism, new age thought, eastern religions and modern psychology fill the minds of many today who are searching in the wrong places for truth. Solomon, one of the wisest men who ever lived, instructed us to seek wisdom as we would seek gold and silver (Proverbs 8). Scripture teaches, "If any of you lack wisdom, let him ask of God, that giveth to all men liberally, and upbraideth not; and it shall be given him" (James 1:5). The university of divine wisdom never closes; it always offers classes to anyone who will come. Alternate answers will not meet the desperate cry arising from every life. The true answers to life's questions come to us through the revelation of the Holy Spirit that requires accepting the sacrifice of Jesus' blood as our only means of redemption from sin.

A most destructive wise man who lives in the presence of the king to influence him is Admatha. His name means *unrestrained* or *without discipline*. We see this influence upon our society as a whole today. Without discipline, men become laws unto themselves, wanting their own ways, which ultimately lead to anarchy. Parents today are encouraged by secular humanists not to discipline their children as the Bible teaches them to do. Without discipline there can be no disciples. The word "disciple" means *a disciplined one whose life is governed by discipline*. A disciple of Christ is one who has found the living truth in the Person of Jesus and is following Him, obeying His law of love. If this unrestrained one dictates our decisions, we can expect to suffer self-destruction, and that much sooner than later.

A very prudent wise man the king employs is one called Tarshish. His name means *It will cause poverty*, or, *will shatter*. He constantly concerns himself with the cost of our decisions, asserting that they could very well bring us to poverty and shatter our relationships and dreams. He would not understand Jesus' declaration, "Blessed are the poor in spirit: for theirs is the kingdom of heaven" (Matt. 5:3). His advice would counter anyone's desire to follow Jesus, for in his opinion the cost of such a decision would be too great to be considered.

A seemingly less obnoxious influence is exerted upon the king by the wise man Meres. His name is interpreted *worthy*, carrying the implication that *You deserve more honor*. The subtlety of this one is perhaps his greatest strength. Who has not heard the voice of this wise man within himself declaring that people don't really appreciate us? We may secretly think, "If they knew who I am, they would heap recognition upon me and give me greater privilege and authority." When those around us concur with that sentiment within us, the potential for conceit and pride is multiplied. This counsel always breeds the ungodly attitude of discontent. Yet Scripture teaches, "godliness with contentment is great gain" (I Tim. 6:6). Following the counsel of Meres will bring, not gain, but loss to our lives.

Marsena is a dangerous wise man to have in the king's court, for his name means *bitter* or *cancerous*. He is a censorious, critical counselor who sees the negative of every situation and declares that we have a right to be bitter. He tempts us especially when painful difficulties have arisen in our lives for which we do not have answers. Bitterness cannot resolve any situation, but can cause much misery to one who yields to its influence. A final wise man, who seems more patronizing than some, is called Memucan, meaning *their poverty*. He asks, "What will your decisions cost others?" Any charitable person would have to listen to such a voice. Our lives do affect those we love and those with whom we associate. Still, we must not allow this voice to influence us in our decision to obey God.

These wise men undoubtedly influenced the king in many of his decisions. In the putting away of Vashti, the rebellious queen, they actually seemed to help him make a right decision. His situation had become so negative that he was willing to make a radical change in his life. It was Mordecai, however, who was responsible for the coming of Esther to the king. The Holy Spirit often takes advantage of crises to help an unregenerate soul decide to receive eternal life. As Mordecai sat at the gates of the king's palace, so does the Holy Spirit watch for an opportunity to offer to the soul that which will really satisfy and bring peace. The Holy Spirit will not overrule the king's will. But He will present to him the beauty of the redeemed life as seen in Esther and allow him to choose the fairest of all.

Esther's name means *renewal* or *light*. Allegorically, she represents the redeemed spirit of a man. The name of Mordecai, the type of the Holy Spirit, means *God enlightens*. Every time there is an Esther to be brought to the throne and a Mordecai who knows the secrets of the kingdom, we must deal with the king's chamberlains and wise men. They are wise in the ways of this world, but know nothing of God's world. Do they sound like any that come around your house? They persuade you to listen to their advice. Their counsel is this: "Decide if you are going to follow the Lamb." "You had better count the cost." "Don't you have rights?" "You are free to choose for yourself." "We don't believe in discipleship and commitment." "If you just follow me, I'll bring you to the top."

In our unregenerate state, we can be thankful for the crisis that brings us to a radical decision to put away Vashti. Her name signifies "Why were you away?" or "Why do you banquet?" She reveals the rebellion and independence of the human spirit that defies even the most sacred relationship. Through the misery created by this rebellious one, the king was given the opportunity to have Esther brought to his side. The faithful Holy Spirit will do the same for every unregenerate soul who comes to such a place of decision, replacing the unrighteous counselors with His wisdom that gives life to all who receive it.

The Church has been tempted to follow many of the worldly counselors we have described. Paul prayed that "...the very God of peace sanctify you wholly;

and I pray God your whole spirit and soul and body be preserved blameless unto the coming of our Lord Jesus Christ" (I Thess. 5:23). The born-again experience makes this purifying process possible. Then the Holy Spirit begins His sanctifying work, cleansing our minds and emotions and enabling us to make decisions according to the will of God. The Kingdom of righteousness, peace and joy in the Holy Ghost is available to us. But we must choose to allow the purifying, changing work of the Holy Spirit as He prepares our hearts to enter the Presence of the King.

The Church is learning what entering the King's Presence involves. We enter His Presence only through true worship that requires separation from the world. We must have a willingness to deny ourselves and to allow brokenness to be a part of our lives. Esther allowed herself to be prepared to enter the presence of the king. We must also allow the painful processes that come to our lives to prepare our hearts to enter the King's Presence.

4

The Preparation of Esther

The Church in Trials

When King Ahasuerus determined to look among the virgins of the land for a queen to replace the rebellious Vashti, Esther was among the beautiful maidens brought to the house of preparation. Choosing a new queen was not a simple matter. There were established procedures to follow.

The maidens were placed in the custody of Hegai, the king's eunuch who was keeper of the women. He gave them the things they needed for their purification, a process required before they could enter the presence of the king. Hegai's name means *meditation*. These young women spent much time alone, separated from home and friends, during their time of preparation. Esther must have had time to think about her family during her days of meditation.

Esther had been orphaned as a child. When her parents died, Mordecai, a near kinsman to Esther, had chosen to adopt her as his daughter and to become responsible for her well-being. Esther's relationship to Mordecai as his adopted daughter played a vital role in the development of her character as a beautiful young woman. Her preparation to enter the presence of the king actually began many years before she was taken to Hegai's house. She had learned to love and trust Mordecai and to follow his instructions explicitly. Her obedience to him eventually determined her destiny and that of her people in the final conflict of this story.

Mordecai's watchful, nurturing care for Esther parallels the relationship of the Holy Spirit to us. God gave the Holy Spirit the task of bringing us into the Presence of our heavenly King. Mordecai sat in the gates of the palace and watched over Esther daily. So does the Holy Spirit sit in our gates and keep His protective vigil over our lives. We have fifteen gates through which we respond to life. We refer to our five senses of touch, taste, smell, hearing and seeing. The same five senses that relate to our bodies relate also to our souls and our spirits. So our tripartite being has fifteen gates that can be influenced for good or evil.

Our obedience to the Holy Spirit is of greater consequence than we may sometimes realize. Obedience is not something we do in spurts, but is an attitude and commitment, the total surrender of a lifetime. We never graduate from the school of obedience; it becomes a lifestyle. Esther had learned a way of life by listening to and obeying Mordecai. Through her obedience she was learning to walk in his ways in preparation to live and reign with the king. Even after she became queen, Esther was aware of Mordecai's moods and still followed his instructions, as later events in the story reveal.

Though Esther was now in the custody of others, Mordecai did not cease his vigil over her life. He concerned himself with Esther's well-being and peace of mind. Every day he walked before the court of the harem to learn how she was faring in the rigors of her preparation for entering the king's presence. His attentiveness must have strengthened Esther's resolve to yield to the lengthy and demanding processes required of her during this time.

The Holy Spirit is the dove of peace. He desires our peace and benefit as Mordecai desired Esther's. Obeying the Holy Spirit brings peace to our hearts. There is no place on earth to find perfect peace except in the perfect will of God. Our submission to His will brings total peace. I do not understand why people are disturbed when they are where God wants them to be. The

will of God is "home sweet home," a place of peace
and happiness. We may shed some tears because of
God's dealings in our lives, but there will be peace in
our spirits. God's Word declares: "Thou wilt keep him
in perfect peace, whose mind is stayed on Thee..."
(Isa. 26:3)

THE TIME ELEMENT

We saw earlier how God uses time to fulfill His
eternal purposes. Esther discovered this truth as it applied to her personal preparation to enter the king's
presence. Though it was an honor to be chosen to be
presented to the king, that fact did not make any easier
the season of preparation required to attain to that
honor. For twelve months the virgins were to be
cloistered away from family and friends and all that
was familiar to them. We can only imagine Esther's
aloneness during this time, attended to by the hands of
strangers. This house of meditation that was required
for the girls' preparation gave them much opportunity
to think about life. The Hebrew word for meditation
carries the connotation of ruminating, which means *to
go over in the mind repeatedly*. We use this same word
to refer to a cow that peacefully chews its cud. It
means *to chew again what has been chewed slightly*. It
also means *to engage in contemplation*.

The time element involving separation and aloneness is part of God's preparation process in our lives.
Special purposes in God require special seasons of

preparation. Who has escaped the inevitable place of aloneness when God has summoned him to come into His Presence? Even if we are not physically alone, there can be a feeling of intense loneliness because of a lack of understanding from people we love and from whom we expect to receive comfort.

It takes time alone in prayer to cultivate a relationship with God. To search the Scriptures and meditate on them requires much time, during which we gain a truer perspective of God and become acquainted with His heart. We are changed as we behold Him in the Word. Too often we are in a hurry; we decide that since we prayed once and nothing "happened," we will not pray again. We must allow God time to prepare our hearts before He brings us into His Presence. If we rebel against His time element, we only succeed in lengthening the preparation process, or perhaps even in thwarting its purpose.

Esther's willingness to submit herself to a lengthy time of preparation revealed the strength of the relationship she had with Mordecai. She had learned to listen to him and to regard his instructions in their home, which prepared her for her destiny as queen. That training helped her to be obedient in all the preparation that the house of Hegai required of her. Esther's life of obedience was the key that brought her into the place of preparation. Her character, formed through years of discipline, was revealed in her present obedience.

The Church is not exempt from the time element of God. God always works according to the "fulness of time" (Gal. 4:4). The Holy Spirit works in the Church to form the character of God in us to be revealed through our obedience. We must yield to the five laws of the dying seed if we are to become the fruit-bearing Christians that God intends us to be (John 12:24). One of those laws involves the time element required for the seed to die.[1]

The seed has a difficult time from the moment it is dropped into the ground until it produces its first fruits. It faces extreme loneliness. If we could hear its voice crying from under the dirt, we would hear that grain asking why it is down there. You don't even see sunshine when you are under the ground, dying. From our hearts comes a plaintive cry. "Why this darkness, and aloneness, and wretchedness that I feel?"

These things must be experienced that we might drop the outer lobe and lose the outer crust. The old lobe must rot so that the new life may come forth. Our flesh life must die so that the life of the spirit can be fruitful. (Even so, the crust of our flesh life is made useful as fertilizer to feed the new life's growth.) The life that springs from the ground is different from that which was planted in the ground. The life of the seed germinates and a new life comes forth.

We must be willing to lose our identity underneath the soil. When the new life of Christ bursts forth from our old shell, people won't see us anymore. They will talk about the King. All we know is the dirt around us and the smell of death upon us. But if we wait for the inevitable results of yielding to the time element, new life will be forthcoming, springing from our death.

THE OIL OF MYRRH

Having yielded to the time element required, Esther encountered other conditions that would bring change to her life. During the first six months of Esther's preparation period, myrrh was the ingredient used in her purification. Myrrh, an oily extract taken from a bush, was used as a healing salve in that day. It was fragrant, but when hardened into kernels, it had a very bitter taste. In Hebrew the word for myrrh means *distilling in drops*. This term gives us the picture of a dispenser automatically dripping the oil of myrrh as it is needed. It suggests to us the testings, brokenness and seasons of weeping during which we need the oil of myrrh to be applied to our lives.

As a chief cosmetic used in the house of preparation, the oil of myrrh represents grace for the dealings of God in our lives. We are made beautiful by the breakings that have brought tears. For those difficult times in our lives there is grace, more grace and much grace to be given upon request. Not by our works of righteousness, but by His grace are we made beautiful. God wants to give us a testimony of His great grace that abounds in our lives.

The suffering that comes into our lives may be caused by physical pain or by emotional or spiritual distress. It may come from people or situations we encounter. As we submit to our personal purification processes, there is a balm of Gilead that God begins to pour into our spirits. When the bitter experiences of suffering come into our lives and we allow the myrrh to be applied, we emerge with a broken and contrite heart. The more our spirits are broken and contrite, the more myrrh God will pour into us.

The Scriptures teach that a broken and contrite heart God will not despise (Ps. 51:17). When God looked down to earth from heaven and asked if He could find a home here, the prophet responded, "What kind of home do You want?" God answered that He would dwell with those of a broken and contrite spirit (Isa. 57:15). What is a broken and contrite spirit? What do we mean by the term *breakings*? The Holy Spirit taught me that it means the surrender of our wills, ways, words, walk, warfare and worship. As we surrender these areas of our lives, we receive the exchanged life. These aspects of our lives are not merely harnessed to the will of God. They must be pulverized, losing all their strength, which is the true definition of contrition. The exchange of our self life for the Christ life is not a simple transaction carried out by the assent of the intellect. It requires dying to our self life. That dying, the loss of the carnal in exchange for the spiritual, causes suffering. The aroma of the oil of myrrh ascending to the throne signifies a life that is broken and contrite. Esther experienced the fragrance and aroma of great grace as she submitted to her purification process.

I had the pleasure of smelling myrrh in the spiritual realm one night. (I have since also smelled the literal fragrance.) After a service in Highpoint, North Carolina, I sat on a front row seat in the church. I did not want to waste the anointing that was hovering in that place. As I was basking in the Presence of God that evening, my spirit ascended and I was not aware of anyone else being there. I heard footsteps and knew someone was walking in the room. I knew it was Jesus, though I hadn't seen His face.

I had preached that night about the cross and the requirement of the gospel that we die to our self life. People had responded with a willingness to be broken; they were willing that the myrrh be a part of their lives. Now, as I sensed the footsteps of Jesus, I began to smell the most beautiful aroma; it was the fragrance of myrrh. He revealed Himself as the broken Christ that I had preached that night—in His hurt love, the love of Calvary.

When I first began to smell the sweet fragrance, I started to cry. I said to Him, "That is myrrh." He replied, "Yes; that is the fragrance of My Presence. That is the fragrance I want you to wear. It is the fragrance that belongs to the anointing. It won't come until the dealings of God work in your life, until the breakings come and tears become a part of your life." When we tune our ears to hear His voice and desire to please Him above everything else, when we focus our eyes on the Holy Spirit and obey Him, His anointing will be ours. The dealings of God will come to our lives to break the pride of our self life. Grace will be poured into us. When we stand in a broken, teachable spirit before people, that anointing will pour out of our brokenness and bring life.

Treatment with the oil of myrrh required obedience, aloneness and submission to the time element. All were part of the preparation needed to enter the presence of the king. Sometimes we find ourselves resisting the dealings of God in our lives. But it is those very dealings that break us, and the myrrh poured into those wounds that makes us beautiful. The breakings bring forth the aroma of grace in our lives. If we are only slightly broken, there will be a limited flow of grace. There must be many breakings in our lives, many strippings when God humbles us in His Presence and pours His grace into us. Each time we respond to our sufferings with greater contrition, He creates greater beauty within us. *Contrition* is a total submissiveness without protest to the will of God. It requires a crushing of the sin nature in us until it resembles the fine dust of baby powder that has been contrited.

SWEET SPICES

During the second six months, Esther's purification process involved the application of sweet spices and cosmetics for women. The sweet spices represented her consecration to the will of God. There is a beauty in a consecrated life that inspires the admiration of others. The life that is submitted to the processes of purification without murmuring or complaining bears a beauty that is supernatural. That beauty can only be received through obedience to the Holy Spirit.

Jesus displayed the epitome of submissive obedience in His relationship with His heavenly Father. Being filled with the Spirit, He never did anything that He did not see the Father doing. Entire nights He spent alone with His Father, always determined to please Him and to fulfill the Father's will. He experienced the loving care of the Father as He consecrated Himself wholly to the will of the Father.

The Church cannot know the visitation of God without submitting to the dealings of God that result in brokenness. Until we wear the fragrance of myrrh, and have the sweet spices of consecration applied to our lives, we cannot be a dwelling place for God. Esther and the other girls were required to be in preparation for one year before appearing before the king. I don't know how long a year is in the sight of God regarding our time of preparation. Perhaps the length of preparation depends upon how well we hear His commands and obey His decrees. The path God chooses for us will be determined according to our submission to the breaking experiences that have come into our lives by His divine appointment. If we have not been willing to endure the dealings of God in our lives, the door will not open for us to be brought into the Presence of the King.

When I speak of coming into the Presence of the King, I am not referring simply to enjoying a time of worship. I believe a time is coming when the body of Christ will come into the King's Presence as we have never known Him before. Those who have been hungry for God and have submitted to His purification processes will come into a relationship with Him that completely satisfies their hearts. Though I do not mean to minimize the precious revelation that we have had of God, I believe the next move of God will bring to the Church a revelation of the Father that we have not yet known. It will be a much greater revelation of God for those who are willing to wear the fragrance of myrrh.

David gives us a beautiful picture of the bridegroom coming with garments that smell of myrrh, aloes and cassia (Ps. 45:8). In that same passage he describes the king's daughter who is all glorious within (v. 13). That inner beauty is wrought by God through the purification processes He ordains to rid us of our self life and sinful ways. Her clothing is of wrought gold and her raiment of fine needlework. As we have seen, gold in Scripture represents the character of God. The fine needlework refers to the intricate workings of God in a life to create the beauty He desires. Piercing needles are painful, but if we escape the painful processes of God we will not have His beauty in our lives. Then we will miss the entrance into His Presence at His appointed time.

Prophetically, Esther's preparation relates to the dealings of God in His Church today, individually and corporately. Those who are willing to follow the Holy Spirit, our heavenly Mordecai, and to submit to the purification processes of the house of preparation, will become a part of the plan of God to choose a bride for His Son. That love relationship is waiting for those who are prepared for it. Obedience is still the key prerequisite for entering this glorious relationship with our King and becoming part of the answer for the deliverance of God's people.

End Notes

1. Dr. Pickett's message, "The Laws of the Dying Seed," is available on cassette tape ($6.00 per copy postpaid) by writing to Dr. Fuchsia Pickett Ministries, 394 Glory Road, Bountville, TN 37617.

5

The Reign of Queen Esther

The Church in Trouble

When it was time for Esther to go in to the presence of the king, she did not of herself require anything to take with her. It was the custom that the girls could choose to take anything they wanted into the presence of the king to enhance their appeal to him. They thought that the more exotic the gifts they brought, the more the king's esteem of them would be raised. His attraction for them would surely be heightened by some elaborate perfume or other sensual object. Yet Esther chose to enter his presence taking with her only what Hegai advised. She did not request anything herself to help her win the king's favor.

Esther's time of preparation had worked beautiful graces in her. God does not capriciously ask us to endure a season of waiting to merely tantalize us. His timing is part of the process of preparation that does a work of grace in us. Esther obtained favor of all who looked upon her simply because of the beauty of her person. Similarly, it is not our talent, background, inheritance, church, our own goodness nor our Bible training that obtains for us the favor of our King. Achievements and works are not items of attraction to Him. Allowing the preparation He prescribes for our lives will create a beauty that satisfies His heart supremely when He looks upon us. Then we will bow at His feet and say, in the words of the old hymn, "Nothing in my hand I bring, Simply to the cross I cling."

> *So Esther was taken unto king Ahasuerus into his house royal in the tenth month, which is the month Tebeth, in the seventh year of his reign. And the king loved Esther above all the women, and she obtained grace and favour in his sight more than all the virgins; so that he set the royal crown upon her head, and made her queen instead of Vashti.* Esther 2:16-17

At the end of Esther's preparation period, the king chose her to become the new queen by the exercise of his free will. Following the allegory of tripartite man, the king's choosing of Esther parallels the experience of being born again. The Holy Spirit took advantage of the dilemma of the king's soul to give him opportunity to put away the rebellious spirit of Vashti and invite Esther to take her place. Esther, the redeemed spirit, took her place in this kingdom, giving the Holy Spirit greater access to the soul.

The goal of the Holy Spirit is to redeem this "mighty one," disarming the power of the flesh and ruling the entire kingdom in righteousness. For that to happen, there will be more conflict, not less, during the reign of lovely Queen Esther. Her coming to the throne does not end the trouble in this kingdom. It only exposes a source of conflict.

Not long after Esther began to reign, the king promoted Haman above all the other princes, and commanded that everyone bow to him and pay him homage. The king and Haman got along well as they cooperated to satisfy their desires to rule. They walked in agreement together to fulfill the plans and wishes of the will, mind and emotions of the kingdom of man. Their need for preeminence and honor characterized their actions and motivated all their thinking. Anyone who did not properly acknowledge the lordship of this king and nobleman, representing so dramatically our soul and our flesh, had to pay the consequences of their wrath.

Haman desires to take preeminence and rule next to the king. The Scriptures teach that the flesh lusts against the spirit and the spirit lusts, or wars, against the flesh (Romans 7). This is a very real conflict that results in the death of one opponent. The spirit and flesh cannot coexist. We must choose to put one to death, or the other will surely die. So the choosing of Esther is the first major step toward the sanctification of the whole man. Being born again brings us under the influence of the Holy Spirit, Who will never bow to the flesh, just as Mordecai refused to bow to Haman.

The Church suffers the same deadly conflict that rages in every born-again Christian, the battle between spirit and flesh. The Church must not bow to the desires of Haman; yet if she does not bow she can expect real trouble. Our great enemies are the world, the flesh and the devil. The Bible teaches us to put on the whole armor of God, that we may fight in this warfare aimed at destroying the purposes of God for His Church. The enemy cannot prevail, for God has determined that He will have a glorious Church (Eph. 5:27). We must decide for ourselves that we will be part of that Church. That decision will require us to take up the warfare against our enemies so that we will not become casualties of this very real conflict.

A closer look at Haman will provide valuable insight for us in understanding the nature of this conflict. The king established Haman's authority over all the princes and commanded that everyone bow to him when in his presence (Esther 3:1-2). Haman, as we have seen, represents the natural man, the self life, the Adamic nature. The name *Haman* means *tumult* or *a razer*. His nature is demanding and ambitious, and he will create conflict whenever his desires are disregarded. When the king, who represents our soul, was born again, receiving a new spirit in Esther, that new life did not affect Haman. Self doesn't change at salvation. On the contrary, Haman's self-assertiveness caused the king to promote him after Esther became queen. Self is the greatest enemy that the redeemed man has. The devil ever seeks to make the believer egocentric. If he can keep man in this condition, he has succeeded in separating him from the power of God. It is the Christ life within us that is the power of God, and Christ-centeredness is the antithesis of self-centeredness.

The Scriptures are clear concerning the ancestry of Haman. He was an Amalekite, a descendant of Esau. Esau, the paternal head of the Amalekites, lightly considered his birthright and foolishly sold it to his brother Jacob. Haman was an Amalekite living in Shushan, the land area that was previously the territory of the Amalekite kingdom. Esau became the adversary of God's people again as satan sought to regain the territory he had lost.

When God commanded Saul to kill Agag, the leader of the Amalekites, along with all the other Amalekites,

Saul disobeyed and kept the "best" of the spoil and
Agag, the leader. Because of his disobedience, Saul
not only lost his kingdom, but an Amalekite killed him
(II Sam. 1:13). How often do we consider the "good"
things in our flesh which God commands must die?
Paul wrote, "In me, that is, in my flesh, dwells no good
thing." Every fleshly drive threatens the life of the
spirit within us. Our self life must be brought to the
cross, where it loses its power to militate against the
purposes of God. When the power of the Holy Spirit is
working in us, we will refuse to bow to our fleshly nature.

"But Mordecai bowed not, nor did him [Haman]
reverence" (Esther 3:2b). This godly man would not
obey the king's decree to honor Haman. The Holy
Spirit refuses to bow or give preeminence to anyone
but God. Mordecai did not bow to Haman because, as
a Jew, he would not pay homage to anyone except
God. A Jew did not bow to any king other than
Jehovah. That was the reason the Babylonian king
threw the three Hebrew children into the fiery furnace.
They refused to bow in worship to a heathen image. It
made no difference if they were beheaded or burned, a
Jew would never bow to a foreign god. Any time a king
tried to become a dictator over a Jew's spiritual wel-
fare, the Hebrew refused to bow to that authority.

So every time Haman walked through the gates of
the palace, Mordecai humiliated him by refusing to

honor him as the king himself had commanded. The Holy Spirit sits in our gates as Mordecai did, requiring us to reckon with Him every time we go in and out of our palaces. If we want our fleshly desires to rule our lives, we will despise this Mordecai, who confronts us with his lack of allegiance to the lordship of our flesh. Haman became infuriated with Mordecai and determined to kill, not only this man, but the entire race he represented. We dare not ignore the power of the fleshly life to carry out its purpose of destruction to all that is spiritual. Until we defeat Haman, he stands next to the throne in authority, with the king himself giving him complete liberty to fulfill his destructive purposes.

Mordecai's refusal to bow so enraged Haman that the Scripture tells us he despised the idea of getting rid of Mordecai alone. His wrath would only be pacified if he could annihilate all the Jews. So he went to the king who had placed his confidence in him and told him that there was a people living in his kingdom whose customs were different: They did not bow to the king. Notice Haman's strategy. He knew that if he told the king he didn't like Mordecai, that would not have impressed the monarch. Instead, Haman persuaded him that this was a group of people who did not obey the laws of the Medes and the Persians. He easily convinced the king that it was not in his best interest to tolerate this people, and the king granted him permission to destroy them. Haman even offered to pay for the destruction of the Hebrews to prove his loyalty to the king, but the king refused the money. He gave Haman his signet ring to help him to carry out his plan.

It is easy to hear our carnal mind reasoning with the king in this situation. "King, you deserve to be honored; you don't deserve to have anyone in your kingdom who doesn't bow to you." The king is easily persuaded of his importance as ruler of his vast kingdom. Haman epitomizes the fleshly desire in us that rivals Mordecai for the rulership of our kingdom. Our house does not belong to Haman or to the wicked king. It belongs to the King of Kings and to Mordecai. God wants us to bow at the feet of Jesus and to love Him with all our heart, our mind, our soul, our body and our strength. We are made for Jesus, the Lover of our souls. When we choose to allow our flesh to rule, it shows our rebellion, loving our flesh more than the true Lover of our souls. Rebellion is carrying on an affair with a foreign lover that doesn't belong to the place God made for our hearts. God declared in Scripture that Amalek was not to be exalted, and it was one of the first nations to be destroyed (Numbers 24). If we do not obey God and destroy the works of the flesh, we can be sure of the destruction of our relationship with God.

Haman did not indict Mordecai personally. He merely indicted a people who were different and, according to him, not loyal to the king. Not many people today would speak against the Holy Spirit. On the contrary, they confess that He is the Third Person of the Trinity. But when He moves in a way contrary to the way they have always done things, they complain and determine not to change the way they have worshiped all these years. In that way, the flesh tries to control and threatens the life of the Holy Spirit in the Church. The Church has often exalted personalities, talents and giftings, and has bowed down to man instead of to God. We have substituted the reasoning of the carnal mind for the wisdom of the Holy Spirit. We wonder why we don't have the Presence of God in our services or the power of God to see lives transformed. It is because we are enthroning Haman and threatening the life of Mordecai who sits in our gates. Both cannot rule. Our flesh often has the preeminence until our spirit begins to grieve and cries out to God for mercy.

HAMAN'S PLOT

> *So Haman said, If it please the king, let it be written that they may be destroyed....And the king gave Haman the signet ring to set a seal on this decree, saying, Do with them as it seemeth good to thee.* Esther 3:9,11

Mordecai put on sackcloth and covered his head with ashes when he learned of the plight of his people. Then he went into the city and cried with a loud and bitter cry. As the decree for the death of the Jews was proclaimed throughout the land, there was great mourning among the Jews, and fasting and weeping. All who walked through the gates of the palace observed these signs of mourning and grief, and Esther's maids came and told her of the state of Mordecai.

When Esther saw his condition it grieved her heart, and she sent raiment to him, which he did not receive. Then she sent a servant to Mordecai to find out why he was mourning.

The Holy Spirit has a mood of weeping that we must learn to recognize if we are to understand the burden of the Lord. He prays in us with groanings that cannot be uttered (Rom. 8:26). Determined to fulfill the will of God, He weeps when we insist on our own will. When Haman comes to us to argue his "rights," he will try to deceive us into siding with him instead of Mordecai. The "rights" of the flesh always threaten the life of the Spirit in us. Haman is subtle. He does not come to us declaring that he is going to destroy us. He comes as our servant to tell us we have rights that some are not recognizing. We deserve honor that we are not receiving. Haman wants position, recognition and honor to make a name for himself. He will use every flimsy excuse in the world and will do it religiously. Haman doesn't speak through strangers, but from the dearest people around us, and from within our own minds and hearts.

My battles have not been with people in the world. My heart has been the battlefield where flesh and spirit meet in deadly conflict. I received my richest training during the few months I studied with a small class of only twelve students. The size of the class did not concern me, because I knew the teacher, Helen Vincent

Washburn, had something I needed. Many people asked me why I was wasting my life in that insignificant classroom in the basement of a church. But I chose to listen to the heavenly Mordecai within me Who told me to stay there until I had learned what He wanted to teach me.

My godly teacher pointed her finger at my face with tears streaming down her cheeks. Her penetrating, deep blue eyes rebuked me as she warned, "You will never be worth the time God has invested in you, nor will you ever answer God's call while you hear the bleating of the sheep in your ears." She was referring to that historical account of the time Saul disobeyed God by saving the best of the spoils and King Agag. She was right, and I ran out of the classroom to the dormitory. There I sprawled on my face, crying out, "Live or die, Agag has to go!" I had not spoken to that teacher, but she had been on her face in prayer at three o'clock in the morning. She prayed over us as though we were the only people in the whole world. God allowed my Haman to be dealt with as I chose the life of the Spirit over the life of the flesh. We must choose to die to the voices of Agag and Haman in our lives, making God's Presence the desire of our hearts. Then we will touch His scepter and request the death of Haman. I can testify that there is nothing and no one worth our missing the will of God for our life. Siding with Haman's strategy to choose our rights is not worth the consequence of losing life in the Presence of the King.

The Church in trouble has to decide if she will compromise and try to allow the flesh and the Spirit to coexist. If she will not compromise, she must face the threatenings of Haman for not bowing to his lordship. The church that does not defeat the flesh life will never know the reality of the Kingdom of God under the authority of the Holy Spirit. Esther shows us the way to dethrone Haman. Through her selflessness and great courage she saved her life and her people.

6

The Courage of Esther

The Church in Threatenings

Mordecai sent word to Esther to make her understand the seriousness of Haman's decree against the Jews. He warned her that she would not survive, though she lived in the king's palace. If she remained silent, she could expect to lose her life and to see her father's house destroyed. Then Mordecai asked a poignant question. *"And who knoweth whether thou art come to the kingdom for such a time as this?"* Understanding the sovereignty of God, Mordecai believed that the whole purpose of Esther's becoming queen might have been to intercede for the people of God to save them from destruction. As we approach the climactic events of this historical episode, let us not be influenced by the fact that we have read the end of the story. Instead, may we capture the depths of this tragic human drama whose outcome depended on the heart decisions made by young Queen Esther.

Esther knew the decree of Haman threatened her life. Her only recourse was to appeal to the king to spare her life and her people. But the decision to make her appeal would put her life equally at risk. According to the law, no one whom the king had not summoned could appear before him, and she had not been summoned for thirty days. Anyone daring to come into the presence of the king otherwise placed his life at the king's mercy, hoping he would extend his golden scepter to him. If he did not, the person was put to death. So death for Esther was certain at the hand of Haman and was possible at the hand of the king. She chose to submit her life again to Mordecai and to abandon herself to the will of God. Mordecai charged Esther to plead for mercy for her people face to face with the king. So Esther called all the Jews in Shushan to join her and her maidens in a three-day fast. Then she courageously declared "...so I will go unto the king, which is not according to the law: *and if I perish, I perish*" (Esther 4:16).

The Church today must come to this abandonment to the will of God that does not cringe at the thought of death. She must throw aside every false hope that she will be spared from the destruction Haman has decreed. In Revelation we read, "And they overcame him by the blood of the Lamb, and by the word of their testimony; and they loved not their lives unto the death" (Rev. 12:11). If the Church is going to be saved from the world system and its philosophies, she must experience a time of brokenness and repentance, sackcloth and ashes, and waiting on our God. The life of the flesh is a deadly enemy to the life of the Spirit. We have the same recourse as Esther if we expect to be spared destruction. We must find the place of humility in fasting and prayer for ourselves and the people of God. She knew what was required to come into the presence of the king. She could only appeal to his mercy to spare her life. One of the first things we learn to ask when we come into the Presence of the King is that we be granted mercy.

IN HIS PRESENCE

Now it came to pass on the third day, that Esther put on her royal apparel, and stood in the inner court of the king's house, over against the king's house: and the king sat upon his royal throne in the royal house, over against the gate of the house. Esther 5:1

On the third day of the fast, Esther dressed in royal splendor. Lamenting and fasting and prayer are part of a process for coming into the Presence of the King. But when we stand in His Presence, we wear the royal apparel we have received from Him. We dress in what pleases Him, coming into His Presence in joyful attire, leaving the weeping outside. When we enter His Presence, it is to invite Him to a banquet we are preparing for Him. The psalmist wrote, "Enter into His gates with thanksgiving, and into His courts with praise: be thankful unto Him, and bless His name" (Ps. 100:4).

Esther first stood in the inner court, waiting for the king to notice her. The three positional verbs that unlock the Book of Ephesians are *sit, walk* and *stand.* Those same words unlock the truths of the Book of Esther. She learned how to sit, to walk, and to stand in the king's presence. The psalmist wrote, "Blessed is the man that walketh not in the counsel of the ungodly, nor standeth in the way of sinners, nor sitteth in the seat of the scornful" (Ps. 1:1). Esther knew when she entered the presence of the king that it was proper to stand quietly, waiting for his acknowledgment of her presence.

When the Lord revealed the message of the Book of Esther to me in a vision, I was standing in the doorway as Queen Esther. I stood almost trembling, yet I was somehow unafraid. I knew I had to stand there until I saw the King's eyes. I can never explain how deeply He wrote on my heart that I must not be taken up with anything around me. I knew I had to look at Him until

His eyes rested upon me. When I was a child, my daddy often guided me with his eyes. He could direct me as to where to sit and how to behave just by the way he looked at me. Esther knew that when she had the king's eyes, they would indicate whether she had obtained his favor.

In the Song of Solomon we read of eyes described as the pool of Heshbon. One characteristic of this pool was its clear, unclouded, pure waters. It was so clear that one could see his complete image when he looked into the pool. Those clear eyes characterized by the pool of Heshbon were the eyes of the bridegroom. Paul wrote, "But we all, with unveiled face beholding as in a mirror the glory of the Lord, are being transformed into the same image from glory to glory…" (2 Cor. 3:18, NAS) When we look into His eyes, He makes our eyes as the pool of Heshbon, clear and pure to reflect His Image. We cannot make our request of the King until we obtain His favor. Eyes are an expression of the heart that reflect our attitudes and reveal our affection.

As Esther stood there hoping the king's heart would respond to her when he saw her, she knew her fate would be signified by whether or not the scepter was raised. We in the United States are not familiar with the beautiful word *scepter* because we are not governed by a king. When I visited England, I went to see the queen's jewels. I was amazed to find that the royal jewels include a crown, an orb, a salt dish and the scepter. The scepter signifies complete authority extended toward a subject. When the king extends his scepter toward you, you have won his favor; whatever you ask will be granted.

> *And it was so, when the king saw Esther the queen standing in the court, that she obtained favour in his sight: and the king held out to Esther the golden sceptre that was in his hand. So Esther drew near, and touched the top of the sceptre.* Esther 5:2

The queen had risked her life and had been granted the favor of the king. As we surrender our lives and everything we have that is precious to us to God, we will find the favor of our King, and our petition will be granted. Scripture teaches us that total surrender wins the heart of our King and causes Him to extend His scepter to us as we stand in His Presence.

When the king extended his scepter, Esther came close enough to touch the top of it. In touching the king's scepter, Esther was expressing her gratitude for his kindness in accepting her. An attitude of thankfulness must be ours as we enter the Presence of the King. True thanksgiving is not simply saying words, it is an outpouring of heart gratitude. It is a beautiful experience when my heart bows in thanksgiving. I know that, although I am not worthy to be in the Presence of the King, He has accepted me. I don't stand in my righteousness, but have obtained His favor.

In touching the scepter, Esther not only expressed her gratitude, but also showed her subjection to the king. Bowing before the King expresses our willingness to hear whatever He says. We must not touch the scepter without a willingness to obey the instruction we hear from the King. Not only would she listen and bow to what he said, but leaving the king's presence, she would do whatever he told her to do. When we know that we are truly subject to our King, we can invite Him to a banquet and He will be delighted to attend.

> *Then said the king unto her, What wilt thou, queen Esther? and what is thy request? it shall be even given thee to the half of the kingdom.* Esther 5:3

I used to think that Esther didn't dare to tell the king what she wanted at first. It seemed to me that her real need was to get rid of Haman, and that instead of expressing that, she invited the king to a banquet. But the Holy Spirit corrected my thinking. According to the king's word, Esther could have had anything that she wanted. She could have requested Haman's death at that moment. She was expressing her real desire to the king when she replied, "If it seem good unto the king, let the king and Haman come this day unto the banquet that I have prepared for him" (Esther 5:4). Esther's heart desire was to have communion with the king at a banquet she prepared for him.

Preparation is always necessary to knowing the King's Presence. Our hearts must be prepared for a banquet of communion before we invite our King to come. Going to church and sitting with our hands folded, waiting for Him to bless us is not enough. We must make preparation to invite the King to a banquet we prepare for Him. Then we decide to bring our Haman with us, fully intending to expose him to the King. Esther knows that the only place Haman can be dealt with is in the presence of the king. Remembering that Haman represents the flesh of man, we must be willing to bring our flesh into the Presence of our King to expose him. We need to take the initiative and decree an obedience for our flesh. It is possible for our inner man to command the outer man to do what God tells us to do. Inviting our Haman to a banquet we have prepared for the King is the first step in our deliverance from the decree of death this flesh life has over us.

There was a time when I did not understand that the King would come to a banquet I prepared for Him. When God began to teach me this principle, I was involved in a large, apparently successful ministry to people. He asked me if I would be willing to leave the outer court and stop ministering to people and minister to Him instead. It was lonely without the crowd. I wept and grieved, thinking my teaching days were finished. He didn't let me think differently until I showed my willingness to stay there at His bidding. Then He made me understand that as I come into His Presence to minister to Him, I am changed through communion with Him. As He fed me, I would become living bread for the people. For many months He required me to come aside with Him alone, and He changed my perspective of ministry. It was life-changing as I began to learn the difference between working for God and having Him work through me.

At midnight on Good Friday of 1966, as I was leaving a church service, the Lord asked me if I was willing to lose myself. He would teach me how to worship Him. He wanted to bring me into His Presence and teach me how to bring others into His Presence in a new way. I did not know before that night that I could "minister to the Lord," though I had ministered to people for many years. But I learned that in divine order, when we come into the Presence of the King, it is our place to provide a banquet for Him.

He said, "Daughter, you have preached a benevolent message from the Scripture: 'I was hungry, and you gave Me nothing to eat; I was thirsty, and you gave Me nothing to drink; I was...in prison, and you did not visit Me' [Matt. 25:42-43, NAS]. That message resulted in ministry to the physical needs of people, which is part of the gospel. Yet I live in My people, the brethren, and I come to church in them, hungry. I live in you, and you must feed Me so I can grow to full stature within you." When I first spoke the words, "Let me feed You, Lord," it sounded like blasphemy to my ears. Then I began to understand that the life of God within me needed to be nourished by time spent in His Presence, in prayer and worship and in the Word.

There is a two-fold way to be changed into the image of God. One way is as we behold Him in the Word; the other is as we receive His life through our worship. Worship is not merely an emotional experience, but a coming into His Presence so that He is able by His Spirit to impart a deposit of His life in us. As we worship God, we feed the life of the Spirit within us and satisfy His heart. As we behold Him in the Word, He takes the pen of the eternal writer and transcribes it on the tablets of our heart. Then we become the living Word. Then it is that we become living epistles, "known and read of all men" (II Cor. 3:2). We cannot live without receiving life from God. My inner man has no other way to live because it is a quickened spirit and must receive that life from God, Who is Spirit. As I behold Him in His Word and worship Him, His life can flow in me.

So Queen Esther prepared a banquet for the king in order to commune with him. She knew the power of life and death were in his hand. And she invited Haman with the intent of exposing his wicked plot in the presence of the king. She knew her appeal could be presented only to the king and was grateful for the mercy she had thus far received. At the banquet the king again offered to grant any petition Esther had, even to half the kingdom. And Esther said again...

If I have found favour in the sight of the king, and if it please the king to grant my petition, and to perform my request, let the king and Haman come to the banquet that I shall prepare for them, and I will do tomorrow as the king hath said. Esther 5:8

Time spent with the king created a desire for more time in his presence. Esther was not in a hurry to disclose her petition, but desired more communion with her king. Of course, all this was preparation for making known her petition in pleading for life for herself and her people.

So it is that as the Church worships in the Presence of the King, our hearts are united with His heart in preparation to make our petitions known to Him. He alone has the power to grant life to us and to redeem us from the threatenings of our enemies.

7

Esther Exposes Haman

The Church in Worship

Haman exulted in his pride when he received a second invitation to dine with the king and queen at a special banquet. He left the palace rejoicing in his honors and privileges, boasting of them to his friends. But when he went through the king's gate and passed Mordecai, indignation filled his heart. He complained vehemently to his wife about Mordecai, and she counseled him to prepare a gallows fifty cubits high on which to hang the Jew. She then advised him to talk with the king the next day about the hanging. Haman liked the idea, and had the scaffold built.

THE KING'S AWAKENING

That night after the first banquet, the king was unable to sleep. He had the chronicles of his kingdom brought to him, and while hearing them read he discovered that a certain man had saved his life and had not been honored for it. Then the king heard someone in the court. When he asked who was there, he found that it was Haman, waiting to talk to him. The king asked him what should be done for the man that the king wished to honor. Presuming that man to be himself, Haman immediately described the way to honor him accordingly. He began to rejoice in the thought that his day of exaltation had come. He would wear the king's crown and royal apparel, and be paraded through the city on the king's horse. Someone would proclaim before him, "Thus shall it be done to the man whom the king delighteth to honour" (Esther 6:9).

Haman always knows what he wants to say, what should be done and how it should be done. He asserts himself because he thinks he is better than others. His main purpose is to destroy Mordecai, or the work of the Spirit. He is very sure he will gain his objective because of his influence with the king. If we are honest, we must admit that the Haman who lives in us very closely resembles this historical Haman.

Haman wanted to wear the king's robe. The law of the land demanded death for anyone who wore a garment that duplicated the color, fabric or style of the king's robe. The only way anyone could wear such a garment was for the king himself to give it to him. The Church can only be robed in righteousness as we come into the King's Presence. We cannot make our own robes to look like His, or allow someone else to dress us. According to Isaiah the prophet, our righteousness is as filthy rags. Haman promoted his honor unlawfully, desiring to wear the king's robe. Yet the flesh will never be clothed with righteousness, for it seeks its own honor, which is the antithesis of righteousness. True repentance brings forth the robe of righteousness, as it did for the prodigal son. The father himself had the best robe brought to be placed on his son when he returned to his house repentant. Our heavenly Father will do the same for His sons who are truly repentant.

Haman not only wanted the king's robe, but his crown as well. Scripturally, many kinds of crowns are given to worthy souls. Among them are a martyr's crown, a soulwinner's crown, an overcomer's crown, a crown of life and a crowning with lovingkindness. These gifts are given from God Himself to His children and will one day be cast at His feet as we worship Him for Who He is. However, Haman wanted the highest crown of the kingdom to be placed upon his head. His desire was to enjoy complete supremacy, even as lucifer desired to dethrone God and to be worshiped. Since satan was cast out of heaven to the earth, he has deceived men into worshiping him. His primary goal is not to make drunkards or harlots of people; that is only a by-product of fallen life. His ultimate intent is to receive the worship that belongs to God alone.

If you want to expose satan, you will find him wherever there are thrones. He lurks around the gate of the throne room because he wants to ascend that throne so he can be worshiped. He did not succeed in getting the Father's throne, but he is determined to get the children's thrones. He is struggling to dethrone Jesus, the rightful Lord of our lives, and to assert his lordship in our minds and hearts. Each of us is responsible to give the crown of honor to our flesh or to yield to the Holy Spirit in this life-and-death struggle.

Haman also wanted to ride on the king's horse. Horses were used to celebrate in a parade of victory, declaring that the battle had been won. When Jesus comes back again He will be riding a white horse with a banner that proclaims, "The Word" (Rev. 19:11-13). The world will know that the Word has triumphed over the flesh and the devil. That ultimate victory for which we are all waiting will be celebrated as the King of Kings rides a horse. That fact adds significance to Haman's desire to feign his victory in the same manner.

HAMAN'S HUMILIATION

In contrast to the aggressive, self-seeking spirit of Haman was Mordecai, sitting in the gate. He had been watchful to protect the kingdom, though he did not yet have his rightful place in it. He was not seeking his own honor, but was always watching and working for the godly rule of peace and righteousness. In the providence of God, the king had been made aware of the nobility of this Mordecai. He was the one deserving of true honor, and was to receive it according to Haman's specifications.

> *Then the king said to Haman, Make haste, and take the apparel and the horse, as thou hast said, and do even so to Mordecai the Jew, that sitteth at the king's gate: let nothing fail of all that thou hast spoken.* Esther 6:10

After Haman paraded this enemy through the streets, he went to his house mourning. We can imagine the supreme humiliation Haman suffered at having to honor Mordecai in the streets of the city. He was angered and shamed to have to exalt this Jew who would bow only to the living God and give honor to no other. The flesh is very predictable in its attitudes and actions, always trying to rule and seeking honor for itself.

The day had come, however, for Mordecai's exaltation. He never exalted himself, and he never honored the flesh. The aim of Mordecai was to exalt the king and to bring the bride into relationship with him. In this same way, the key ministry of the Holy Spirit is to exalt Jesus in the Church and to bring the Church and bride home for our Lord. In type, the beautiful story of

Rebekah and Isaac (Genesis 24) shows the servant going in search of a bride for the son. It teaches us the work of the Holy Spirit in the earth: to build the Kingdom of God within our hearts and to fit our hearts for eternity. His assignment is to bring the Church home, and out of that Church to find a bride for our Lord. We should evaluate our work for God by whether or not we are exalting Jesus. If we are not, it is the flesh that is working rather than the Spirit.

Haman's goal was to reign alongside the king and to destroy everyone who didn't give him due honor. That is why the day the king chose to honor Mordecai was a day of extreme humiliation for Haman. He had little space to grieve, however, for it was time for the second banquet that Esther had prepared for him and the king. The timely honoring of Mordecai must have given Esther courage as she prepared to expose her enemy in the king's presence.

HAMAN EXPOSED

The second banquet Esther had prepared for the king was a banquet of drink. She chose to commune with him over a banquet of wine, which represents the life of the Spirit as opposed to works. She was in the presence of the king to touch his heart and to please him as his queen. It is obvious that the king responded positively to her attentions, for he repeated his desire to know her petition. His mind and interests, which had not been with her for several weeks, were turned to her again as she presented herself to him in this time of communion.

Though God is never unmindful of us, it is still true that He delights in our coming to Him in true communion and fellowship, preparing a banquet of worship and love for Him, before we address our requests to Him. In our times of loving Him, His heart is stirred to grant us our petitions. We are admonished in Scripture to make our requests known to Him with thanksgiving (Phil. 4:6). It was during this time of communing that the king again asked Esther what her petition was.

Esther responded by saying, "If I have found favour in thy sight, O King..." That must be our concern when we begin to petition our King: that we have found favor in His sight. She continued, "...and if it please the king, let my life be given me at my petition, and my people at my request" (Esther 7:3). Her cry, simply put, was, "Life me and life my people, or we will die!" In stating her petition, Esther acknowledged that her life could come only from the king. There must come a time in our lives when everything else has been swallowed up and we have only one motivating desire. The psalmist cried, "One thing have I desired of the Lord, that will I seek after; that I may dwell in the house of the Lord all the days of my life..." (Ps. 27:4) He wanted to dwell in the Presence of the Lord forever. Esther wanted to dwell with her king, but she could no

longer coexist with her adversary, the wicked Haman
who had decreed her death. We must realize that all the
desires of the flesh militate against the life of the Spirit
within us. Then we will lay them aside with only one
request remaining: "Life me and life my people."

As Esther proceeded to explain her plight and that
of her people, the king became angry and asked who
dared plot such a wicked crime. Then Esther answered,
"The adversary and enemy is this wicked Haman" (Esther 7:6). Mordecai had fulfilled his assignment of in-
forming Esther regarding who the real adversary was,
and now in the presence of the king she was able to expose him with knowledge. Unless the Holy Spirit
reveals the truth concerning who Haman really is, we
won't *want* him to be destroyed. Esther had learned
that Haman was not the loyal representative of the king
that he pretended to be. She had fasted and prayed and
made preparation to come into the presence of the king
with full knowledge of the decree of death over her
life. That is the determination we must have when we
come into the Presence of the King: to be rid of our
flesh life and to receive life from Him.

God's plan for the Church in the last days is to bring
us into the Presence of the King in worship, to know
Him and love Him, and to exchange our flesh life for
His life. Paul declared that he "suffered the loss of all
things" and counted them but dung in order to win
Christ (Phil. 3:8-10). He expressed his desire for the

righteousness that comes through faith in Christ, concluding with his heartfelt cry, "that I might know Him" (v. 10). To know Christ and to be clothed with His righteousness is to be stripped of our flesh life by our choice. If we keep trying to save our flesh life, we will lose our life in God. If, however, we keep yielding our will to Him, we will continue to receive His life, which is eternal. The decree of death will be overturned for us and we will know great rejoicing in the Presence of the King.

The king was greatly angered when he learned the truth of Haman's evil plot to kill his queen and all her people; so much so that when the king's servants told him of the scaffold that had been built for Mordecai and suggested that Haman be hanged there instead, he commanded it to be done. Only then was his wrath pacified.

On that day did king Ahasuerus give the house of Haman the Jews' enemy to Esther. And Mordecai came before the king; for Esther had told what he was unto her. Esther 8:1

When the time had come for Esther to reveal her identity along with that of Mordecai and his relationship to her, Esther gave Mordecai his rightful place in the kingdom. Then the king gave to Mordecai the ring of authority that he had previously given to Haman. "And Esther set Mordecai over the house of Haman" (Esther 8:2).

We must become as offended with our flesh life as this king was with Haman. When we realize what wickedness it intends for the life of God within us, we will respond as vehemently against it as did the king. Then the true government of God can be established in our lives and we can live in peace. That is what we do when we yield to the Holy Spirit and allow Him to rule in our lives. We make that choice in the Presence of the King, where Haman has been exposed and his death decreed. In our walk with God, we cannot expect to be untroubled by Haman, our flesh life, except as we maintain our commitment to the will of the Holy Spirit. We must cultivate a relationship with Him as the One who rules over us.

When we receive life of the King, He will write His Word on our hearts to change the decrees of Haman against us. He sends His Word to heal us and transform us. We will know the truth and the truth will set us free (John 8:32). Every ordinance that is written against us for our destruction has been rewritten by the blood of the Lamb, and as we apply that blood to our lives, we are cleansed and transformed into His Image.

Then there must be the undoing of the "mischief of Haman the Agagite" (Esther 8:3). Esther pleaded with the king to put away the ordinance that he had devised to put all the Jews to death. She could not endure seeing the evil destruction that was decreed for her people. She cried, "If I have found favor in thy sight, O king, and if it please the king, let my life be given me at my petition, and my people at my request." Her strong desire for her people was revealed in her plea for life for herself and for them.

In the place of worship, the Church will receive life and find deliverance from Haman. That is why God wants to bring the Church into a new place of worshiping the Lamb, beholding Him in His beauty and in His power to change our lives. The reality of Haman also explains why the carnal minds of religious men oppose the idea of worship. As long as the flesh life rules, it will seek honor for itself and will try to destroy the life of the Spirit which finds satisfaction in worshiping the Lamb.

Asking God to "life us and life our people" will result in a church that has been impregnated with the living Word (seed) of God and is alive to the Presence and purposes of God. This is not the same as asking for church growth, for having large numbers of people does not mean we will have more of the Presence of God. However, having people who are living under the rule of the Holy Spirit and receiving their life from the King will draw others who desire the same quality of life in God they see in the Church. Many people living in Shushan became Jews because of the fear of the Jews that came upon them when Mordecai began to rule. Life begets life, and the Church can expect to be fruitful in building the Kingdom of God when she has truly conceived life in the King's Presence.

8

Kingdom Rule Established

The Church Triumphant

Only after our own life is established in God can we intercede for others who are doomed to destruction by the enemy.

> *And Esther spake yet again before the king, and fell down at his feet, and besought him with tears to put away the mischief of Haman the Agagite, and his device that he had devised against the Jews.* Esther 8:3

As we have seen, the king's wrath was kindled when he realized that the enemy had touched the queen and the people of God. Because of the law that did not allow the king's decree to be reversed, the king told Esther and Mordecai to write out a new decree against their enemies.

The new decree would prove to be a higher law to supersede the first law. Though it did not set aside the first law, it gave recourse to the Jews to nullify its death-dealing effect on them. In the same way, the law of love is higher than the law of Moses. Though Jesus came to fulfill the law, He did that through the power of the higher law of love. The new commandment He gave was that we love one another and so fulfill the law of Christ. In fulfilling that commandment, the law becomes powerless to condemn us.

The new decree was to be sealed with the king's signet ring, and gave power to the Jews to defend themselves against their enemies in the day of battle. Even when the wrath of God is kindled against our enemies, He will still involve us in conquering them. The decree we initiate against our enemies will be stamped by the authority of the King. Then a battle must be waged, as was required for Esther's people to triumph over their enemies.

We learn, with the psalmist David, that God will teach us to war and give us great victory in the day of battle (Ps. 18:28-43). To the Church has been given the power and authority to destroy principalities in the heavenly realm. Through worship, the heavenlies above us can be cleansed of enemy powers. The heavenly realm is our rightful territory, for we have been seated in heavenly places in Christ Jesus (Eph. 2:6). We must learn how to bring down strongholds and every high thing that exalts itself against the knowledge of God, being ready to avenge all disobedience when our obedience is fulfilled (II Cor. 10:4-6).

Esther's intercession for her people, because of Haman's wicked devices, is paralleled in the Church today by our intercessions against the works of the flesh, which are often energized by the devil. The work of Haman in the Church must be destroyed, for he determines to destroy the Church. The works of the flesh as listed in Galatians chapter five include immorality, impurity, sensuality, idolatry, witchcraft, hatred, strife, jealousy, outbursts of anger, disputes, dissensions, factions, envying, drunkenness, carousing and other things like these (vv. 19-21). Wherever we find these evils, Haman, with his destructive power, is in charge.

The Old Testament reveals eleven sins toward God that bring His wrath upon man. God opens up the earth and sends people to hell alive or breaks them out with leprosy to punish these sins. One is touching God's anointed people. It is dangerous to oppose or do damage to God's anointed. The Lord declares, "Touch not Mine anointed, and do My prophets no harm" (I Chron. 16:22). I used to wonder why Miriam broke out with leprosy just because she disagreed with her brother Moses about whom he was going to marry. She may have had a right to disagree with her brother at home, because she was part of his earthly family. But she took her complaint against God's anointed one to the "church." It caused trouble in the camp, and God cursed her with leprosy. He lets leprosy come when we cause dissension in the camp. God will not let people go into the next great move of God who touch His program, His purposes (plan), His prophets or His prophecy.

Esther set Mordecai over the house of Haman to establish the rule of the righteous kingdom. In our lives and churches, we must declare, "Blessed Holy Spirit, this is Your temple. Everything we have is Yours; we have no reason to live except You. We will not give any room for the flesh to rule within us or among us." That is dedication. The Church will prosper under the rule of our heavenly Mordecai. If we will totally commit our lives to the Holy Spirit, we will discover that He wears the ring and has access to the throne to seal any petition we ask. And His laws cannot be reversed.

Does the devil ever tell you God doesn't answer your prayers? Satan is the biggest liar there ever was, the father of lies. Sometimes our prayers are not answered because we ask amiss or we have violated a principle God has required concerning prayer. But if our prayer is sealed by the Holy Spirit's signet ring, it will not be turned away. Mordecai was given the king's ring to authorize an answer and a law, and no man could reverse the words thus sealed. Even if supernatural forces try to hinder the answer to our prayers, we will still receive an answer. Scripture reveals that the prophet Daniel fasted and prayed for twenty-one days without receiving an answer to his petition. Then an angel appeared to him with the answer and explained that there had been supernatural resistance to his prayers that had delayed his coming (Daniel 10). God always wins those battles if we keep our place in prayer before Him. When God enters a battle, the victory is assured, and we are made more than conquerors in Him.

Committing our lives completely to the Holy Spirit gives us true position, authority and wealth. I would not stoop to be the Queen of England. That is not spoken in arrogance; I know that position would never be offered to me. But if it were, I would not stoop to it, because I would rather be an ambassadress of my King than to rule over a few people. I don't have to wear crowns of diamonds and jewels; I have crowns that will fade not away. I don't have to have a scepter to be locked away in a glass case; I have a scepter I can use. I don't have to put on a robe for festival days; I have that robe to wear every day as I am clothed in His righteousness. Why should I ask to be a political leader over people when God has made me a leader to carry the gospel? That is the highest calling on earth. We cannot fulfill our calling unless we are willing to give Mordecai the whole house.

Esther's request that the king take care of the results of Haman reminds me of a passage of Scripture found in First John that is more precious to me than any other when I go through tests and trials. "For this purpose the Son of God was manifested, that He might destroy the works of the devil" (I John 3:8). "For this purpose" I apply to whatever I am going through at the time, and declare the destruction of that enemy by the power of Jesus. The word "destroy" is the Greek word *louso*, which means *that He might undo, outdo and overdo everything the devil has ever done*. Because of Jesus' death and resurrection, no matter what difficulties we go through, we do not have to lose ground. We come to the other side of the trial with the enemy undone and outdone. Haman and all those who may be against us have been defeated by the cross. If we choose to die to self, let Mordecai wear the ring and give Him the house, then God will take care of us.

A FINAL LOOK AT SHUSHAN

The name *Shushan* has greater significance than we have yet discovered. The word means *the abode of the holy*. There was a literal palace of Shushan, where the king had his throne and where these historical events happened. Shushan was where Esther gave Mordecai full authority over her house, and where Haman was overthrown. Figuratively, the palace is where the King lives. God wants our hearts to be the palace of Shushan, where the Holy Spirit rules and the flesh is overthrown.

The word *Shushan* contains the Hebrew *h* sound. In Hebrew or Greek the letter *h* is not written; it is only pronounced in speaking when indicated by a written accent. For example, the word for "temple" is *ieron* and means "an ordinary building made of wood and stone." If we wanted to change that word to mean "God's temple," we would put an accent called a rough breathing mark in front of it. To change an *ieron* into a *'ieron* (/hieron/), we must have breath. There is no life without breath. Only after Adam was breathed upon by God did he become a living soul.

That is what has happened all the way through the Book. Abram's name was changed to Abra*ham*. Sarai was changed to Sar*ah*. When God touched a life, He breathed into it His life, and He changed the person's name accordingly. That rough breathing breathed all the way down to the day of Pentecost. The believers were sitting in the upper room—in an *ieron*—in one accord, and there came the sound of a mighty rushing, breathing, wind. The Spirit sat upon each person with tongues of fire, representing God's holiness. God is holy, and is seeking a holy people in whom to dwell. With His fire He writes on us, His living stones, with His living Word. And His holy nature and life become our life. He wants to live in a holy place, in Shushan, in our hearts. God wants a home into which He can breathe His holiness to perfect it. He wants us to praise Him with hallelujahs. "Alleluia" is written with a rough breathing mark, so we say *Hallelujah*—we are rejoicing that He is breathing His life into us.

Shushan was where the decree was written that gave the Jews, Esther's people, the right to defend themselves against their enemies. God fought with them, and they won complete victory over their enemies in that holy place that was under the rule of Mordecai. In our lives, that is where we will be granted favor and receive the answer to our petitions. Out of the heart that has been breathed upon by the Presence of the King, decrees will be issued that bring victory over the enemy. Life will come forth from that kind of prayer and that kind of living. A life that has become a temple for the Presence of the King will be used to bring forth life in others.

In typology, the city throughout Scripture represents the Church. Jesus called us a city set on a hill. When Mordecai went out of the palace dressed in fine linen and purple, the city of Shushan rejoiced. When the Holy Spirit takes His rightful place in the Church, it is time to rejoice. Singing, shouting and dancing are wonderful expressions of rejoicing in the Church. There is celebration when we come into the house and have victory over the flesh. When the feast day comes there is no more sitting in sackcloth and ashes. We have been in the Presence of the King; our petition has been answered, and decrees have been made. Haman has been hanged, and the gallows are going to take care of his generations. Our life is turned from sorrow to joy, from mourning to feasting and sending portions to others. The Church can look forward to a time of celebration when her enemies have been defeated through the power of the Holy Spirit as He takes His rightful place in our hearts.

A decree is stronger than a petition; it cannot be reversed. When the decree goes forth from the palace of Shushan, sealed by Mordecai and at the request of Esther, she knows the desire of her heart will be granted. There are decrees yet to be made for the Church as she learns to walk in the ways of Esther and comes into the King's Presence. There are petitions yet to be answered, requests still to be granted. When God issues a decree, we can say, "Move over, devil, demons and everyone else. This decree is coming to pass!"

As we have seen God's design for the Church in the Book of Esther, we might be inclined to ask where the Church finds herself today regarding the processes of God. I believe the greatest revelation of God that man has ever known is yet to come. The Church is going to know the King as we never thought we could know Him. The Book of Esther speaks prophetically to the triumphant, glorious Church without spot or wrinkle that will know the ultimate reign of her heavenly Mordecai and the destruction of her enemies. God's eternal plan[1] as revealed to Paul, that which had been hidden in God from the beginning of the world, will be realized in its fulness. Paul declared that he was given grace to preach the unsearchable riches of Christ, "to the intent that now unto the principalities and powers in heavenly places might be known by the *Church* the manifold wisdom of God, according to the eternal purpose which he purposed in Christ Jesus our Lord" (Eph. 3:10-11).

Paul explained that God gave gifts of ministries to the church "for the perfecting of the saints...till we all come in the unity of the faith, and of the knowledge of the Son of God, unto a perfect man, unto the measure of the stature of the fulness of Christ" (Eph. 4:12-13). We do not see the Church today in her ultimate triumph over her enemies. However, she is under the watchful eye of Mordecai, the Holy Spirit who is giving revelation and exposing the real enemy of our souls. Our hope for victory over our enemies lies in our obedience to the Holy Spirit as He faithfully maintains His vigil to bring us to safety.

God, who dwells in eternity, is not limited as we are. He need not apply only one process at a time to our lives. In some ways we may feel we are in the place of preparation in which Esther found herself, alone and secluded, meditating and submitting to special disciplines. In other ways, we may realize the joy of communing in His Presence in worship at the banquet we prepare for our King. And we may find ourselves in the day of battle decreed for us against particular enemies who are vying for our souls as we petition our King to life us and life our people. It is vital that we stay in constant communication with the Holy Spirit, so that we will not be deceived by Haman, a flesh life so cunning that it threatens our life in God.

As the Church humbles herself to fast and pray and present herself before the King, she will know true worship and experience ultimate victory over her enemies. To that end, may we join our hearts in Esther's longing cry, "If it please the King, and if I have found favor in Thy sight, life me and life my people!" I pray that the Holy Spirit will give this cry to many hearts who have been brought to the Kingdom *"for such a time as this. "*

End Notes

1. See Pickett, *God's Dream* op.cit., for further explanation.

Tapes

FTP 001	If We Confess Our Sins
FTP 002	Voice in the Wilderness
FTP 003	Ten Virgins
FTP 004	Four Winds of God
FTP 005	Good Samaritan
FTP 006	Good Shepherd #1
FTP 007	Good Shepherd #2
FTP 008	Doctrine of Hell
FTP 009	PEACE—What Brings It?
FTP 010	God's "I Wills"
FTP 011	God's Bomb Shelter #1
FTP 012	God's Bomb Shelter #2
FTP 013	Blood Covenant #1
FTP 015	Blood Covenant #3
FTP 016	Testing Hour for the Church #1
FTP 017	Testing Hour for the Church #2
FTP 018	In Adam vs In Christ
FTP 019	Predestination #1
FTP 020	Predestination #2
FTP 021	Eating His Flesh and Drinking His Blood
FTP 022	Powers of the Holy Spirit
FTP 023	The Holy Anointing Oil
FTP 024	Moods of the Holy Spirit
FTP 025	Danger of Shortcuts
FTP 026	Be Ye Steadfast #1
FTP 027	Be Ye Steadfast #2
FTP 028-FTP 030, 3 tapes	Seven Offices of the Holy Spirit
FTP 031	Nobleman's Son
FTP 032	Two Lives
FTP 033	Stop Signs to Hell
FTP 034-FTP 043, 10 tapes	Book of Jude
FTP 044	Two Tongues in Acts Two
FTP 045	Sermon on the Mount #1
FTP 046	Sermon on the Mount #2
FTP 047-FTP 049, 3 tapes	How to Know the Voice of God
FTP 050	Liberty in Service #1
FTP 051	Liberty in Service #2
FTP 052-FTP 058, 7 tapes	Book of Ruth
FTP 059	Rev. Fuchsia T. Pickett's Testimony
FTP 060	Consider the Lilies
FTP 061	The Church in These Last Hours
FTP 062-FTP 067, 6 tapes	How to Search the Scripture
FTP 068-FTP 073, 6 tapes	Trees of the Bible
FTP 074-FTP 082, 9 tapes	The Family Life
FTP 083	Women in the Ministry #1
FTP 084	Women in the Ministry #2
FTP 086	Fasting (Isaiah 58) #1
FTP 087	Fasting (Isaiah 58) #2
FTP 088	The Anointing of the Holy Spirit #1
FTP 089	The Anointing of the Holy Spirit #2
FTP 090	Pilgrims on the Way Home
FTP 091	Seven Things God Hates
FTP 092	Lord, Keep Me From Wandering
FTP 093-FTP 098, 6 tapes	Priesthood
FTP 099	The Word

FTP 100	Do You Know God? #1
FTP 101	Do You Know God? #2
FTP 102	Awakened Heart of the Bride
FTP 103	Bride and Her Gifts
FTP 104	He Took Her
FTP 105	Ruth in Review
FTP 106	Famine in the Land
FTP 107	Seeking a Bride
FTP 108	Gleening in the Field
FTP 109	Watchcare of Ruth
FTP 110-FTP 112, 3 tapes	Psalm 23
FTP 113	Overcoming Our Confessions #1
FTP 114	Overcoming Our Confessions #2
FTP 115-FTP 117, 3 tapes	Can God Be Known?
FTP 118-FTP 122, 5 tapes	Christian Growth
FTP 123	Praise
FTP 124	Principles of Light
FTP 125	Soul Help
FTP 126	Be Ye Filled With the Spirit
FTP 127-FTP 130, 4 tapes	What God Says About Our Children
FTP 131-FTP 134, 4 tapes	Four Aspects of Worship
FTP 135-FTP 138, 4 tapes	Leprosy
FTP 139	God's Protecting Altars
FTP 140	Divine Longing
FTP 141	Victorious Living
FTP 142	Hidden Ones
FTP 143	Sonship
FTP 144	Names of God
FTP 145	The Word—Spiritual Food
FTP 146	God Calls Abraham
FTP 147	Little Foxes That Spoil the Vine
FTP 148	Resurrection
FTP 149	Inspired Voice
FTP 150	What to Remember at Communion
FTP 151	Training Our Children
FTP 152	Overcoming Our Nearer Kinsman
FTP 153	Our Words
FTP 154	Believer Priest
FTP 155	Manifestations of the Sons of God
FTP 156	Entering His Gates
FTP 157	Faith: Substance and Evidence
FTP 158	Wedding of Christ and His Bride
FTP 159	Presentation of Levites
FTP 160	The Valley of Baca
FTP 163	The Just Shall Live by Faith
FTP 164	Seven Appearances of Jesus
FTP 165	What the Holy Spirit Has Come to Do
FTP 166	Characteristics of Maturity
FTP 167	Feast of Unleavened Bread
FTP 168	The Spirit of the Elder Brother
FTP 169	Appearances of Christ
FTP 170	Thou Hast Put Gladness in My Heart
FTP 171	Open Thou Mine Eyes
FTP 172	Poured Out Life
FTP 173	The Values of Worship
FTP 174	Seeking and Finding Your Beloved
FTP 175	Why We Take Communion
FTP 176	Salvation
FTP 177	Keeping Back Part of the Price
FTP 178	Being Brought Out
FTP 179	Exhortations From Proverbs
FTP 180	Rejoice in the Lord Always
FTP 181	Thou Whom My Soul Loveth
FTP 182	There are No Shortcuts
FTP 183	Anointing

FTP 184	The Day of Vengeance #1
FTP 185	The Day of Vengeance #2
FTP 186-FTP 196, 11 tapes	I Peter
FTP 197-FTP 201, 5 tapes	The Lost Things
FTP 202	Remember
FTP 203-FTP 207, 5 tapes	Submission
FTP 208	Loneliness of Jesus
FTP 209	And the Walls Were Built
FTP 210	The Glory Cloud #1
FTP 211	The Glory Cloud #2
FTP 212	Fear Thou Not
FTP 213-FTP 216, 4 tapes	Faith
FTP 217	Let Us Consider One Another
FTP 218	Does God Ever Change His Mind?
FTP 219	Humility
FTP 220	What the Bible Says About the Word
FTP 221	The Fire of God Reveals It
FTP 222	Can God Tell Me What to Do? #1
FTP 223	Can God Tell Me What to Do? #2
FTP 224	Under Shepherd
FTP 225	Worship Interaction #1
FTP 226	Worship Interaction #2
FTP 227	Why Are We Afraid of God's Presence?
FTP 228	The Model Prayer #1
FTP 229	The Model Prayer #2
FTP 230	In Decency and in Order
FTP 231	Reverence
FTP 232	Spiritual Blessings in Zion
FTP 233-FTP 235, 3 tapes	Ten Steps to Victory
FTP 236	The Peril of Keeping Back
FTP 237	Characteristics of a True Prophet
FTP 238	Anointing—Vial or Horn
FTP 239	Anointed
FTP 240	Ezekiel's Victory #1
FTP 241	Ezekiel's Victory #2
FTP 242	God Led Them Not by Way of the Philistines
FTP 243	Hezekiah's Crisis
FTP 244	God's Hiding Place #1
FTP 245	God's Hiding Place #2
FTP 246	Lordship
FTP 247	Hannah's Prayer #1
FTP 248	Hannah's Prayer #2
FTP 249	True Worship #1
FTP 250	True Worship #2
FTP 251	Be Ye Thankful #1
FTP 252	Be Ye Thankful #2
FTP 253-FTP 255, 3 tapes	Five Fold Will of God
FTP 256-FTP 263, 8 tapes	The Fear of God
FTP 264	Let Us #1
FTP 265	Let Us #2
FTP 266	Sins Toward God #1
FTP 267	Sins Toward God #2
FTP 268-FTP 274, 7 tapes	God's Call for Mighty Men
FTP 275	What Constitutes a Call #1
FTP 276	What Constitutes a Call #2
FTP 277	The Message of Grace
FTP 278-FTP 286, 9 tapes	Hosea
FTP 287	Our Personal Attitude Toward God
FTP 288-FTP 291, 4 tapes	God's Financial Plan
FTP 292-FTP 295, 4 tapes	Joel
FTP 296-FTP 308, 13 tapes	God's Order of Worship
FTP 309	To the Faithful #1
FTP 310	To the Faithful #2
FTP 311	His Ground Work or Communication
FTP 312	Cease Not to Pray

FTP 313	As Christ Sees the Church
FTP 314	Psalm 34, I Will Bless the Lord #1
FTP 315	Psalm 34, I Will Bless the Lord #2
FTP 316	Keys to the Kingdom
FTP 317	The Bible—God's Message to Us
FTP 318	Ministry of Exhortation
FTP 319	Prayer
FTP 320	Keeping Undisturbed Peace #1
FTP 321	Keeping Undisturbed Peace #2
FTP 322	Feast of the Passover #1
FTP 323	Feast of the Passover #2
FTP 324	Seven Steps God's Word Takes in Us
FTP 325	The Holy Spirit in Ephesians #1
FTP 326	The Holy Spirit in Ephesians #2
FTP 327	Six Cities of Refuge
FTP 328-FTP 330, 3 tapes	Fellowship With God
FTP 331	Blessed Possession
FTP 332-FTP 334, 3 tapes	Discipleship
FTP 335	Leadership (Titus) #1
FTP 336	Leadership (Titus) #2
FTP 337	Your Place is a Spiritual Ministry
FTP 338	Presumptuous Sin—Not Working
FTP 339-FTP 342, 4 tapes	Prayer—II Chron. 7:14
FTP 343	Glorify God in Our Lives
FTP 344-FTP 346, 3 tapes	The Moods of the Spirit
FTP 347-FTP 349, 3 tapes	The Fasted Life (Isaiah 58)
FTP 350-FTP 352, 3 tapes	Defilement by Evil Reports
FTP 353-FTP 364, 12 tapes	He That Overcometh
FTP 365	Joshua: Called and Equipped #1
FTP 366	Joshua: Called and Equipped #2
FTP 367	Dare to Do Right
FTP 368	The New Birth
FTP 369	The Ark of the Covenant #1
FTP 370	The Ark of the Covenant #2
FTP 371	The Promise of His Presence
FTP 373	Principles of Church Growth #1
FTP 374	Principles of Church Growth #2
FTP 375	Principles of Christian Growth
FTP 376	God For, In, and Through Us
FTP 377	Blessings of the Promise
FTP 378	The Birth of the Church
FTP 379-FTP 381, 3 tapes	Consecration
FTP 382	While It Was Yet Dark
FTP 383	Blessings for Obedience
FTP 384	The Lame Prince
FTP 385	Women of Praise
FTP 386	The Happy Man #1
FTP 387	The Happy Man #2
FTP 388	Relationships of the Believer
FTP 389	Possessing the Land
FTP 390	Building Trust #1
FTP 391	Building Trust #2
FTP 392	Prayers of the Holy Spirit
FTP 393	Accepted in the Beloved
FTP 394	Five Things God Uses
FTP 395	Open Doors to Deeper Spiritual Life
FTP 396	Qualifications of a Prophet
FTP 397	An Unusual Storm
FTP 398	The Blood
FTP 399	Bless the Lord O My Soul #1
FTP 400	Bless the Lord O My Soul #2
FTP 401	Restoration #1
FTP 402	Restoration #2
FTP 403	The Planning of the Lord
FTP 404	God is Building a Temple

FTP 405	Building the Temple
FTP 406	A Place to Offer Incense
FTP 407	Discover the Reality of Faith
FTP 408	Four Areas of Unity
FTP 409-FTP 412, 4 tapes	God's Predestined Plan
FTP 413	Faith
FTP 414	The Object of our Faith
FTP 415	The Way of the Transgressor #1
FTP 416	The Way of the Transgressor #2
FTP 418	Profitable Worship
FTP 419	Four Areas of Authority
FTP 420	Let My People Go
FTP 421	Faith
FTP 422	Repentance
FTP 423	The Subject of the Ear
FTP 424	Zion #1
FTP 425	Zion #2
FTP 426-FTP 430, 5 tapes	The Restoration of Naomi
FTP 441-0FTP 443, 3 tapes	Unfeigned Love of the Brethren
FTP 444	Promises #1
FTP 445	Promises #2
FTP 446	Mount Zion #1
FTP 447	Mount Zion #2
FTP 448	Purpose of the Ego #1
FTP 449	Purpose of the Ego #2
FTP 450	Seven Wonders of the Resurrection
FTP 451	Fitness for Service #1
FTP 452	Fitness for Service #2
FTP 453	Faithfulness (Prov. 20:5, 6)
FTP 454-FTP 459, 6 tapes	Doctrine of Deliverance
FTP 565-FTP 570, 6 tapes	Extensive Study of the Seven Offices of the Holy Spirit
FTP 571	To Whom Much is Given, Much is Required
FTP 572	The Holy Spirit's Purpose #1
FTP 573	The Holy Spirit's Purpose #2
FTP 574	The Powers of the Holy Spirit
FTP 575-FTP 577, 3 tapes	Save Yourself From Today's Corrupt Generation
FTP 578	Ruth, Famine in the Land
FTP 579	Ruth, Our Advocate, Not Adversary
FTP 580	Ruth, The Gleaner
FTP 581	Ruth, Boaz the Redeemer
FTP 582	Ruth, Kinsman, Bridegroom and Restorer
FTP 583-FTP 587, 5 tapes	The Spirit of Elijah, the Double Portion
FTP 588	Maturity, Church Growing Up
FTP 589-FTP 591, 3 tapes	The Parable of the Four Kinds of Lost People, Luke 15, Prophetic
FTP 592-FTP 596, 5 tapes	Every Sheep Needs a Sheep Fold, the Church
FTP 597-FTP 602, 6 tapes	Marriage Seminar
FTP 603	The Church of this Hour #1
FTP 604	The Church of this Hour #2
FTP 605	Seven Realms of Authority in God
FTP 606	Authority of the Word
FTP 607	Authority of the Conscience
FTP 608	Authority of Civil Government
FTP 609	Authority of Employer and Employee
FTP 610	Authority of the Church
FTP 611	Authority of the Home
FTP 612	Worship, an Attitude Expressed #1
FTP 613	Worship, an Attitude Expressed #2
FTP 614	Principles of His Word
FTP 615	Women Moving Forth
FTP 616	Leadership #1
FTP 617	Leadership #2
FTP 618	Prejudice Has Got to Go
FTP 619	Woman, Restored to Her Inheritance
FTP 621	The Divine Destiny of the Church
FTP 624-FTP 626, 3 tapes	The New Generation, Prophetic

FTP 627	The Prerequisites for a Double Anointing
FTP 628	Being Established in the House of God
FTP 629	Spiritual Maturity
FTP 630	Contending for the Glory
FTP 631	The Seven Realms of Prayer in James
FTP 632	Saved From This Corrupt Generation, Character
FTP 633-FTP 636, 4 tapes	God's Financial Plan
FTP 637	Is Speaking in Tongues Scriptural?
FTP 638	Worship and God's Eternal Plan
FTP 639	Pure Spiritual Worship #1
FTP 640	Pure Spiritual Worship #2
FTP 641	Spiritual Maturity, Adulthood
FTP 642	Principles for Success in Life
FTP 643	A Family Affair
FTP 644	What is the Church? #1
FTP 645	What is the Church? #2
FTP 646	Revival is Coming to the Church #1
FTP 647	Revival is Coming to the Church #2
FTP 648	Functioning as a Priest (Evening Sacrifice)
FTP 649	Every Sheep Needs a Sheepfold (Summary)
FTP 650	The Holy Spirit, the Third Godhead
FTP 651-FTP 658, 8 tapes	Covenant, in the Blood
FTP 659	In All Things—Give Thanks
FTP 660	The Ministry of Singing
FTP 661	The Sheepfold is for You
FTP 662	What Purpose Does
FTP 663	Restoring the Purposes for Man
FTP 664	Restoring Standards in Women
FTP 665	Purposes of God #1
FTP 666	Purposes of God #2
FTP 667	The Spirit of the Servant
FTP 668	Who is the Church?
FTP 669	Repentance—What Is It?
FTP 670	Thirty-One Kings: The Self Life
FTP 671-FTP 673, 3 tapes	Profitable Values of Worship
FTP 674-FTP 678, 5 tapes	The Called Woman
FTP 679	The Rising of the River of God
FTP 680	Walking in the Spirit #1
FTP 681	Walking in the Spirit #2
FTP 682	Revival: Return from Wasted Gifts
FTP 683	God's Voice to the Church
FTP 684	Delivering the Church to Hear God's Word
FTP 685	Everyone Is Called #1
FTP 686	Everyone Is Called #2
FTP 687	Hurt Love
FTP 688-FTP 690, 3 tapes	Digging for Silver: Reading Out Instead of Reading In
FTP 691	Five Questions of Life #1
FTP 692	Five Questions of Life #2
FTP 693-FTP 698, 6 tapes	Esther
FTP 699	The Journey for Elijah's Mantle

Dr. Fuchsia T. Pickett
c/o Shekinah Church Ministries
394 Glory Road
Blountville, TN 37617
(615) 323-2242

Tapes are $5.00 each.

Please make all checks payable to Dr. Fuchsia T. Pickett.

Please add 15% for shipping costs in the United States.
Please add 25% for shipping costs outside of the States.

Study Books

Outline Studies and Manuals

Child Study	$10.00
Esther	10.00
Holy Anointing Oil	4.00
Holy Spirit	10.00
How to Search the Scriptures	10.00
Job	5.00
Leviticus	4.00
Proverbs and Ecclesiastes	7.00
Psalms	6.00
Romans	6.00
Ruth	5.00
Scriptural Study of Five Senses	7.00
Scripture Numerics	6.00
Song of Solomon	5.00
The Anointing	5.00
The Names of God	5.00
The Good Shepherd	5.00
What God's Word Says about Hell	5.00